ACTING ONE

ACTING ONE

ROBERT COHEN

University of California at Irvine

Mayfield Publishing Company

Library of Congress Catalog Card Number: 83-062822
International Standard Book Number: 0-87484-669-2

Sponsoring editor: C. Lansing Hays
Manuscript editor: Carol L. King
Managing editor: Pat Herbst
Art director: Nancy Sears
Designer: Gary Head
Cover designer: Gary Head
Production manager: Cathy Willkie
Compositor: Auto-Graphics

Credits

Pages 42, 71, 135–36, 169 Excerpts from *Death of a Salesman* by Arthur Miller.
Copyright 1949 by Arthur Miller. Copyright renewed © 1976 by Arthur
Miller. Reprinted by permission of Viking Penguin Inc.

Pages 56–57 From *A View from the Bridge* by Arthur Miller. Copyright © 1955,
1957, 1960 by Arthur Miller. Copyright renewed © 1983 by Arthur Miller.
Reprinted by permission of Viking Penguin Inc.

Pages 57–58 Edward Albee, from *Who's Afraid of Virginia Woolf?* Copyright ©
1962 by Edward Albee. Reprinted with the permission of Atheneum
Publishers.

Pages 121, 179 Excerpts from *Betrayal* by Harold Pinter. Copyright © 1978
by Harold Pinter. Reprinted by permission of Grove Press, Inc.

Pages 135, 169, 172–74, 187–88 From *The Glass Managerie*, by Tennessee
Williams. Copyright 1945 by Tennessee Williams and Edwina D. Williams
and renewed 1973 by Tennessee Williams. Reprinted by permission of Ran-
dom House, Inc.

Pages 160–61 Reprinted by permission of Hill and Wang, a division of Far-
rar, Straus and Giroux, Inc. Excerpt from *The Rimers of Eldritch* by Lanford
Wilson. Copyright © 1967 by Lanford Wilson.

Contents

Lesson 15: Using the Voice   117

Lesson 16: The Actor's Body   125

Lesson 17: Voice and Body Integration   133

Preface

This book is expressly intended for the beginning acting student. The twenty-four lessons comprise basic material for what could be a one-year or two-year course in acting fundamentals. The amount of time needed to "cover" them will vary to the degree proficiency is sought or expected, for while the material is presented as an introduction to acting, these are the fundamentals that professional actors spend their lives exploring and perfecting. None of these twenty-four lessons can ever be fully learned, not even in a lifetime.

Except for a comment in the afterword ("L'Envoi"), matters of characterization and style are not covered because these are not beginning subjects in acting. Young actors may wish to leap into the classics, and into the extremes of farce and tragedy, well before they have even begun to master the basics of talking, listening, tactical interplay, physicalizing, building scenes, and making good choices. The fundamentals, however, should be set down first. What is in these pages will hold true for Shakespearean acting, for comedy acting, or for television acting; these lessons should serve as a basis for all advanced acting skills. Get a good handle on these twenty-four lessons—on the fundamentals of acting—and you will be able to move into more advanced acting problems with confidence.

There are many exercises in the first half of the book; there are fewer in the latter half, where it is expected that the student will be working on scenes from plays. Suggestions for choosing those scenes and for choosing roles are given in Lesson 13. In general, you are advised to find dramatic material from your own time and culture, and characters close to you in age and essential experience.

On several occasions, I have referred to "the young actor," or "beginning actors," with the general implication being that young beginners don't really know what they're doing. Let me apologize in advance for any hurt feelings. On the other hand, most young actors *don't* really know what they're doing, for the simple reason that you cannot see yourself or hear yourself while you're acting, and young actors rarely have enough experience to achieve the objectivity about their performance as veteran professionals do. The young actor may feel something, and feel that he or she feels something, and get quite satisfied if not overjoyed at the intensity of that feeling, without coming within miles of the intensity a more experienced actor would achieve with the same material. In fact, it is very helpful for the beginner to remember that he or she *is* a beginner: Not a great deal need be expected right away, and the best way to begin to act is one step at a time. This book is designed to start that process and carry the beginner into some fairly advanced steps.

The last section of this book, on acting technique, involves some topics not always taught in a beginning acting class. Technique is not always taught because it often proves difficult for young actors to understand how acting can involve emotional and psychological reality and controlled acting "technique" at the same time. It can. Indeed, all fine actors are able to integrate the emotions in a role with a technical ability to perform the role. It is true that some actors (usually American) worry more about feelings, and some actors (usually British or French) worry more about technique, but you do not need to make a choice. There is nothing at all inconsistent between deep and honest emotional responsiveness on the one hand, and a superior acting technique on the other. In every section of this book, I have tried to indicate the honest relationships between genuine feeling and controlled acting technique, and between human reality and the art of the theatre.

I have tried to use ordinary terminology throughout this text. Acting books, including some of my own, have often wrestled uncomfortably with semantics; acting discussions are often mired in semantic quarrels of bewildering complexity. This confusion is perhaps understandable since acting has given the world its jargon for both psychology (*role playing, acting out*) and philosophy (*tragedy, persona,* and the like). Therefore I have stayed with words long in the theatrical lexicon (words which themselves are not precisely defined in all cases), except that I sometimes use *victory* when others use *intention,* and I have used the acronym *VOTE* to denote Victory, Obstacle, Tactics, and Expectation.

I have also kept this book as free as possible from considerations of theory. Students looking for a more theoretical basis for the lessons in this text might wish to explore them in my *Acting Power* (Mayfield, 1978). That book (which *does* deal with characterization and style) conceptualizes a comprehensive system of acting, which might serve as a sequel to this volume.

Finally, no one is more aware than I that acting cannot be taught by a book. Acting can most certainly be taught—and the change over the past two decades in American acting has largely been the result of an explosion of actor-training nationwide—but the key ingredient in actor-teaching is the teacher. I have tried to keep this book open-ended and suggestive rather than narrow and prescriptive, so that it might stimulate, not stultify, the crucial work of the classroom. Acting and actor-training are individual arts within a collective and collaborative craft process. The actor must find his or her way into the self, as well as into the craft, for the art of the theatre is made out of both ingredients. This book is blind to its readers' individualities; it teaches only as interpreted and implemented by you, the actor, or you, the teacher. I have tried to leave as much room as possible for that interaction, which I value as highly as any in the arts.

R. C.

Acknowledgments

The author and publisher wish to acknowledge the assistance of the following acting teachers who reviewed the manuscript at different stages: Carla Meyer and Mary Anne McGarry of the University of California at Irvine; Joseph H. Conger III of the University of Florida; Robert D. Dunkerly of Clark County Community College (Nevada); Roger Hall of James Madison University; Jerry Krasser of the University of Connecticut; David Knight of the University of Illinois at Urbana-Champaign; Randy Wonzong of California State University, Chico; and Leigh A. Woods of Indiana University.

The author also wishes to acknowledge—with special gratitude —Lorna Cohen, for her expert critical assistance, and the acting students at the University of California at Irvine, for not taking anything for granted.

ACTING ONE

Introduction: Preparation for Acting

Can acting be taught?

Yes, of course acting can be taught. In the United States, acting is taught regularly in literally thousands of colleges, conservatories, workshops, and professional studios. Virtually all young actors coming into the profession in the present era have studied acting in some formal manner, and many professional actors continue their training for years beyond their successful entry into the profession. So acting is not only taught, it is *learned*.

Of course, reading any certain list of books, or studying with any particular teacher or teachers, or enrolling in any particular training program, will not guarantee that you will become a great actor, or even a fair one. Fine acting demands a rare combination of talents: intelligence, imagination, psychological freedom, physical dexterity, vocal strength and flexibility, emotional depth, and an ability to learn from mistakes, criticism, and observation. It also requires certain personal prowess, which might appear from time to time as wit, charm, self-confidence, assuredness, honesty, audacity, charisma, passionate intensity, and compelling candor. These cannot be taught, directly, in anything resembling their entirety: They are acquired, if at all, as much through life experience as by training for the stage.

What can be taught, therefore, is a *beginning* to the art of acting. This is something more than merely pointing you at the stage, and something less than giving you a fully codified set of rules and regulations. It is a method of helping you to get the most out of yourself, and to train your acting "instrument"— primarily your voice and body—into a more workable, more exciting, apparatus. And it is a method that will help you learn from life and apply what you learn to the art of translating life into art: the art of the theatre. Providing this beginning is the goal of this book.

In the first lesson,* you will begin acting; in the second lesson you will be acting with an acting partner in a scene. You do not need previous stage experience to accomplish the tasks set forth in either those or the subsequent exercises, which are designed to proceed by steps toward a specified goal. There are, however, some preliminary things you might want to know before the first lesson.

Relaxation

Every actor knows the importance of relaxation, for it is the necessary starting place for acting. Relaxation is both physical and mental; it allows the body to respond freshly and the mind to create spontaneously. A relaxed actor can do anything; a tense actor is always constrained.

Relaxation may not be forced, but it can be induced or self-induced. Simple stretching exercises—rolling the head in large circles left and right; bending the body forward and back; and moving the fingers, hands, arms, and legs in figure-eight patterns—are excellent warm-up techniques that both tone body muscles and release physical tensions. Bouncing lightly on the balls of the feet; vigorously shaking the arms, hands, face, and torso; and rapidly shadowboxing or rope-jumping also limber and relax the body. Virtually all actors develop physical regimens of exercises like these to use before rehearsals and performances, and you should too. Many acting classes begin with such warm-ups; if yours doesn't, you can do your own warm-up beforehand.

Mental relaxation is a matter of putting out of mind the day-

---

*Chapters in this book are organized as individual lessons, although a class may wish to stay with one lesson for several sessions.

to-day affairs of life so that you can concentrate more directly and fully on the problems of acting and on the situation of the characters you will play. Inasmuch as acting is, among other things, a complex mental activity, the more freedom you have from your own daily preoccupations, the more deeply you will be able to involve yourself with your acting situation, even during periods of extreme stress in your personal life. Physical exercise is often a help to achieving this mental relaxation; so are meditation, yoga, thinking about pleasant images, or "playing" soothing music in your head. One of the best ways of achieving mental relaxation in an acting class is simply to look around you and study what you see. What color are the walls? How many people are in the class? Does your teacher wear contact lenses? Are the other students as nervous as you? Who brought their books to class today? Since most mental tension comes from thinking about ourselves (and how we might be failing to "measure up"), thinking about other people helps us to relax and put the world in a better perspective.

Relaxation is the starting point for acting, not the ending point. Don't ever confuse relaxation with "not thinking." Relaxation is not stupor; it is a state of openness and receptivity to your surroundings—a state unmarked by extreme preoccupation or worry. Go ahead and think all you want, but don't burrow into your thoughts and dwell on yourself. Relax with your eyes wide open, your senses fully awake, and with the idea of taking in all you can.

Trust

Trust is also a precondition for acting. Because acting is something you do with, and in front of, other people, anxiety about those people can eat into your ability to act. Trust, like relaxation, cannot be forced, but you can't sit around waiting for it to arrive, either. Trust is a mutual relationship between you and your fellow actor-students—a relationship marked by giving, sharing, and common concern.

You must take the initiative here, because isolation and apathy invest the first classroom meeting with deadly inertia, and only the determined efforts of you and your fellows will break down the walls of carefully nurtured egotism and suspicion that characterize most groups of arbitrarily gathered strangers. If you can find your acting partner interesting, it will make you interested and interesting; if you find your partner fascinating, it will make you fascinated and fascinating. It is to *your advantage* to seek out what is admirable and wonderful in your fellow actors, the qualities that will make them prized companions and colleagues, and will make you a lively partner, dramatically engaged with them.

A word about competition: The theatre *is* a highly competitive business at the upper levels, which means that you will need companions and colleagues all the more. The intensely personal moments that characterize the greatest performances rarely come forth in a climate of contention or antagonism, or through the isolation of seemingly self-sufficient individual actors. Rapport between actors, developed through trusting ensemble work, is the context of fine performance.

Actor-trust means, at bottom, that you are comfortable with your fellows and they with you. It is the feeling that you can make a fool of yourself without embarrassment and can be emotionally open without getting stepped on. Acting exposes personal vulnerabilities (good acting does, anyway). An atmosphere of trust ensures that those exposures are not callously rubbed raw—that indeed they will become, if anything, therapeutic rather than humiliating and enjoyable rather than discouraging.

Trust develops first out of self-confidence and out of shared activities among the acting group. Trust exercises and games are often used; even children's games are frequently brought into classes or rehearsals by teachers and directors sensitive to the need for mutual trust. Pure socializing has its important place in the work of actors, both in class and in the professional world. Mutual massage or mutual back rubs are also beneficial, both for trust and for relaxation. An excellent basic warm-up, involving both, is the following "spine lengthening" exercise adapted from the Alexander technique.

EXERCISE 1

SPINE LENGTHENING

Pair with a partner. One person lies down on a mat, face up, knees raised. The other gently pulls the supine actor's head away from the torso, tilting the chin down slightly at the same time. Going around the supine body, the "massaging" actor gently pulls one limb at a time away from the torso center, pulling along the limb, and then at the extremities, returning to the head after each limb.

At the end of the massage, the supine actor is lifted to an erect position, his or her head is lifted up and away one last time, and the actors reverse positions. This exercise induces a sense of well-being in addition to relaxation and trust; each actor will feel about two inches taller at the end of it.

Neither trust nor relaxation comes about automatically, and for some people neither will come easily at all. Each of us brings different fears and tensions into our work. In general, the more you can focus away from yourself, the more you can recognize the uniqueness and beauty of the persons around you, the more you can respond to the world with wonder rather than with irritation and envy, the more you will be in the creative state that will permit you to act deeply, fully, and with spirit.

Discipline

It goes without saying that an actor must be a disciplined artist. Inasmuch as the theatre is a collaborative art, discipline is essential to the effectiveness of the collaboration. Without discipline, trust disappears. If you can't trust your fellow actor to show up for rehearsal, you can't trust her or him to be sensitive to your feelings.

As a result, theatre artists must be particularly punctual and responsible, must meet all their obligations on time (and *precisely* on time), and must be fully prepared to expend their energies in the pursuit of high standards of artistic effort. That "the show must go on" is a well-known cliché does not detract from its serious importance in the theatre world. Theatre is not a casual activity, and the intensity of the theatrical experience is made possible only by the dedication and commitment of theatre artists to collaborate fully and responsibly with each other on a continuing basis. Discipline makes you someone who can be counted upon, and it makes you able to count upon the commitment of others. There is no better place to start learning artistic discipline than in an acting class.

Criticism

Every actor, from the beginner to the veteran professional, must learn to come to grips with criticism. There is no way around it. Criticism comes from instructors, fellow students, audiences, directors, the press, neighbors, parents, friends, competitors, and avowed enemies. Some is constructive, some instructive, some destructive, and some entirely beside the point. Some you will find useful; some you will find inane; some you will inevitably find "unfair." And let's make no mistake about it: Criticism hurts. Anybody who says it doesn't is either a fool or a liar.

The reason criticism hurts the actor more than it hurts other artists is that the "art" of the actor comes directly out of the actor himself or herself; therefore, criticism of the actor usually takes the form of criticism of the actor's voice, movement, feelings (or seeming lack of feelings), expression, or personality. Some so-called criticisms of acting published in widely read magazines take the form of vitriolic attacks on an actor's personal appearance or mannerisms. It is understandable, therefore, that actors in general tend to take criticism personally—and that's why it hurts.

The best way to relate to criticism of your work is to profit from it. Inasmuch as you are a beginner, you must realize that you have much to learn and that persons with some experience in the theatre can be of great help to you. While well-intended and constructive criticism is obviously going to be the most helpful to you, you can learn from callous criticism as well—as long as you filter it properly. The important thing is not to take criticism *too* personally, and not to waste a lot of time defending yourself. In the long run, it means little if the criticism is "fair" or "unfair." If you can learn from it, use it. If you can't learn from it, forget it. All criticism is subjective in the final analysis, and you're not going to please everybody. You should be aiming at steady growth, greater comfort onstage, and greater freedom to go out on one emotional limb after another. Any suggestions or critiques that you can turn to your advantage are not only to be dealt with—they should be sought after with persistence. The finest actors do not seek to avoid criticism; they solicit it.

Freedom

Finally, the actor must learn to be free—free from physical and psychological inhibition—and must learn to enjoy that freedom. The actor must be free to think, feel, touch, and be touched. Above all, the actor's imagination must be unhindered. Relaxation, trust, discipline, and an effective response to criticism all play a part in this—relaxation and trust because they promote uninhibited interaction, discipline because it establishes a limit to gratuitous encroachment of the actor's physical privacy (preventing, for example, unwarranted sexual groping) and a response to criticism that allows the actor to grow, not shrivel, from his or her experience.

The free actor can imagine *anything*. Fantasy is the actor's playground; unbridled fantasy is the prerequisite to playing Romeo or Juliet, George or Martha. An actor afraid to fantasize, afraid to imagine the unimaginable, is an actor unacceptably bound to a narrow spectrum of emotional life. Plays and scenes may be outwardly mild; inwardly they are usually stormy and violent. The actor's mind must be able to play freely with the inner turmoil of the character: The actor's mind must be open to lust, terror, joy, and exaltation by turns—and must be open to playing the actions that emanate from those mental states. Acting is emotionally risky. Indeed, one of the joys of acting is in taking those risks. The exercises and suggestions that follow in this book, and experience that will ensue in any acting class, will lead into these emotionally risky areas. An actor obdurately refusing to follow that lead—an actor who, instead, retreats behind a fixed image of himself or herself—is not free to act.

Preparation

You may begin to study acting at any age. Indeed, the study of acting is invariably a prerequisite to the study of other theatre arts, such as directing; it is also a useful preparation for public speaking, politics, law, business, and any profession where self-expression and communication are important. But there are some useful things that you can do or study before beginning to act. Dance, in any fashion, is most helpful to the beginning actor because it teaches a physical mode of performance. Athletics also provides a good background for acting, because of the energy it demands and because of the public nature of its exhibition. Singing, poetry reading (and writing), and storytelling are exceptionally helpful because they involve language and performance and getting at the heart of feelings in a constructive way. Reading (novels, plays, and biographies) helps the young actor to understand the complexities of human life, including varieties of human experience not immediately observable in the actor's environment. And of course, theatregoing is a prime preparation for acting: seeing the potentials of performance, and seeing the work of accomplished actors first-hand.

Summary

The precursors to acting—relaxation, trust, discipline, the response to criticism, freedom to act, and prior preparation—do not simply appear on command; nor need you have them in your hip pocket before your first class in acting. They are developed continually in a young actor's work, and they need refreshing throughout an actor's career. They will stand you in good stead whether you become an actor or not, for they are also useful preparations for the interactions of daily life: for relationships of every order, whether personal or professional. And they are the sort of basic goals you should check yourself out on regularly as you pursue your studies toward artistic advancement in the theatre or elsewhere.

PART ONE

The Actor's Approach

cting is a process involving certain transformations: A person is transformed into an actor; an actor is transformed into a character. This process is not sudden or magical (although it may at times appear to be both); rather it is gradual and deliberate.

"The actor's approach" is the series of steps the actor takes in that process. They are steps of exploring, feeling, trying, and doing; together they comprise a set of experiences. Every actor, from the beginner to the veteran professional, goes through these experiences. Every actor re-creates the process of acting with every performance.

"The actor's approach," therefore, is a process of self-transformation—of moving out of oneself and getting into a role or into a work of art. It is a series of first steps that, like all first steps, are very challenging.

Victory and Obstacle

Fundamental Principles

There are two fundamental principles in acting. The first is that the actor must always play toward a *victory*. The second is that the actor must always play against an *obstacle*. The victory (often called an "objective" or an "intention") is what the character wants. The obstacle is whatever stands in the character's way. The extent to which a character is seen pursuing a victory against an obstacle is the extent to which acting is dramatic (as opposed to demonstrative) and dynamic (as opposed to static).

Some simple exercises demonstrate the principle of reaching for a purpose.

EXERCISE 1–1
REACHING

Stand on the right foot; reach as high as you can with your left hand. Reverse: Stand on your left foot and reach with your right hand.

By itself, reaching is not an acting exercise. It is merely a physical exercise, or a calisthenic.

EXERCISE 1–2

REACHING FOR VICTORY

Imagine that there is something you greatly desire above your head:
a beautiful jewel, or a bowl of strawberries, or the key to your true
love's heart. Now, reach again!

When you are reaching for victory, your action is purposeful.
You reach farther, more intently, more energetically. You reach
so hard that you pull yourself off balance; you bounce on the
balls of your feet. You are not merely following an instruction;
you are trying to do something. You are intent upon winning an
objective; you want something. All those words—*purposeful, doing, trying, intent, winning, objective, want*—are useful in describing
the concept of playing for victory. The actor's quest for victory
makes action acting rather than demonstrating, and makes behavior dynamic rather than static.

In reaching, you are working against an obstacle: your own
physical limitations. You can stretch only so far against the pull
of gravity. Now intensify that obstacle:

EXERCISE 1–3

OVERCOMING AN OBSTACLE

Imagine that you are sick to your stomach and fearful of losing control
of your bowels. Reach up as in Exercise 1–2—only the more you
reach, the sicker you feel. The more excited you get at reaching for
your bowl of strawberries, the more fearful you become that you will
publicly embarrass yourself.

In Exercise 1–3, your simple act of reaching has become an
emotionally complex experience, even profound. You are acting.

There is no exercise, no acting challenge that cannot be seen
as a confrontation between an obstacle and an actor's quest for
victory. The job of the actor is to find such victories and obstacles in his or her roles and even in calisthenics and training
exercises. Finding victories and obstacles sometimes involves research, and it always involves imagination. Frequently, imagina-

tion, properly focused, is all that is needed to transform simple, everyday acts into acting.

Imagination is the breeding ground for fantasy, and an actor's fantasy is often the source of his or her most compelling victories and obstacles. What did you think when you read "the key to your true love's heart"? Did you take that literally or figuratively? Would the image of Rapunzel in her tower prison or Robert Redford in chains have made you reach higher and harder? The actor's job is not just to find victories and obstacles, but to *create* them—and to create them with such vividness and enthusiasm that they can lead to an exciting and clearly defined performance, even in a simple exercise.

Self-Consciousness

If playing toward victories and playing against obstacles are the fundamental principles of acting, self-consciousness is the actor's greatest enemy. Standing up and being observed, being "on display" for the presumably critical eyes of others, is a terrifying prospect to most of us.

EXERCISE 1–4

DOING VS. BEING

Do the following actions in order. Allow thirty seconds for each numbered command.

1. Stand up in front of the group.

2. Be dignified

3. Look sexy.

4. Relax.

5. Count the number of men you see.

6. Count the number of women faster than you counted the men. If you succeed, you'll win a prize!

Chances are that the first two minutes of that exercise were agonizing. Being publicly commanded to "be dignified" or "look sexy" fills us with terror; how certainly we will fail! And how can we relax with all those people looking at us? How can we *really*

relax—on cue? But counting the men—that's *doing* something;
the focus moves away from us and onto the watchers. And
counting the women—fast, so as to win a prize (even an imaginary prize)—that's *energetic* doing; that's even almost fun!

The actor cannot simply "be" something or somebody onstage, or simply "look" a certain way without being acutely self-
conscious, unbearably self-aware of "being" or "looking." Nor
can the actor be ordered to relax, because relaxing—real relaxing—means not worrying about obeying anybody's orders! The
only way for an actor to avoid self-consciousness—and to truly
relax—is to *do* something. And the more actors feel they are
doing something *important* (as, for example, trying to win a
prize), the more they relax into the task and think about things
other than themselves.

Projection

Self-consciousness is your focus on yourself; projection is your
focus on others, on the outside world, and your efforts to
project your concerns outside yourself. Projection is also your
ability to project your voice, to be heard by others. Projection,
therefore, is basically the opposite of self-consciousness; it is the
ability to escape the prison of yourself (self-doubt, self-indul-
gence, selfishness) and to enter into active, productive social
intercourse. Every actor must learn this skill quite thoroughly.

EXERCISE 1–5

RESONATING

Do the following actions in order.

1. Face the wall and say "ahhhhhh."
2. Recognize that sound is simply the vibration of molecules. Face the
   wall, say "ahhhhhh," and feel the vibration in your throat.
3. Recognize that sound *resonates* and that sound may set up sympathetic vibrations in other objects. Face the wall, say "ahhhhhhh,"
   and *try to make the molecules in the wall vibrate in harmony with
   your voice.*

The three steps in Exercise 1–5 lead you from self-consciousness to projection. In the first, you are simply making sound. In the second, you are making sound with a purpose: to feel your own vibration. In the third, you are making sound with a purpose that *extends beyond yourself:* In other words, you are projecting your sound purposefully; you are seeking a victory (trying to make the wall vibrate) and struggling against an obstacle (the firmness of the wall). It does not matter if the wall vibrates or not. (Actually, the wall does vibrate, but there's no way you can measure this vibration.) The point is that you have created a victory, using a real object (the wall), your voice, and your imagination.

Did your voice change on the third step? Of course it did. It became louder, more resonant, and more forceful. Chances are that you opened your jaw wider, dropped your Adam's apple lower in your throat, and straightened your posture. You may not know it, but these are exactly what a voice teacher would instruct you to do, and you have done it without thinking about anything except vibrating a wall!

EXERCISE 1–6

RESONATING (A CONTINUATION)

Pair with a partner and space yourself away from others as much as possible. By turns, say "ahhhhhh" to the partner with the intended victory of *vibrating your partner's spine with the sound of your voice.* With your fingers, feel your partner's spine to see if you can feel the actual vibrations. Try different ranges of your vocal pitch, different kinds of vocal sounds, and different positions of your body. Try to feel the vibrations as much as you possibly can.

In Exercise 1–6 you are projecting sound not to a wall but to another person. Moreover, you are trying to sense the physical effects of that projection. Your concentration has gone entirely from the sound of your voice to the physical effect your voice has on your partner, and now your consciousness is not self-directed but other-directed. This exercise has led you to a moment—however simple—of "pure" acting: person-to-person communication at the most fundamental level.

Some acting moments in plays are precisely this: one character holding, cuddling, or embracing another, saying "ahhhhhh" as a way to lull the other character into relaxing, or into a romantic mood, or to settle the other character's nerves. Or, the "ahhhhhh" could be an exclamation, accompanied by a raised sword, as Macbeth draws on Macduff, attempting (as a victory) to frighten him into submission. Not all acting involves "lines," but all acting does involve person-to-person communication, at either the verbal or the nonverbal level.

In playing a role, of course, the actor must project more than just sound. Words, gestures, ideas, feelings, commands, personality: These are among the intangibles that the actor must convey to other actors, and to the "back of the house"—that is, the audience. These projections all enter into the stream of communication that every actor both generates and receives; projections are the means by which actors involve themselves with the activity around them—and turn their focus outward, away from self-conscious self-absorption.

EXERCISE 1–7
VICTORIES

Do the following tasks. Afterward, define the victory, define the obstacle, and discuss the degree to which your involvement in each task "projected yourself" into the world outside yourself and dispelled your self-consciousness.

1. Untie and remove your partner's shoes.

2. Find the 126th word on page 58 of this book.

3. Balance this book on your partner's head.

4. Find the wall or piece of furniture or other object that best resonates with the sound of your voice.

5. Find the best pitch of your voice to resonate that which you found in item 4.

6. Neaten your corner of the classroom.

7. Move people from one corner of the classroom to another.

Summary

The actor always plays toward a victory and against an obstacle. Concentration on *achieving* the victory reduces the actor's self-consciousness; moreover, it demands that the actor *project* by focusing on something or someone. The mutual projection between actors—a person-to-person communication—is the foundation of all acting, even the most complex or most highly stylized.

Acting with the "Other"

The Other

In most plays, the actors do not try to resonate walls; they try to have an impact on other people. Usually those other people are the other characters in the play. For the purposes of acting class, the "other" is your acting partner.

Probing deeply into other people is one of the essential tasks of the actor. This does not necessarily mean long talks into the night, social involvements, mutual therapy sessions, or the baring of personal secrets; it certainly does not mean forcing confessions or outside relationships on other actors. It does mean a willingness to look clearly and directly at your acting partner, and to take in *the whole person* with whom you are acting.

EXERCISE 2–1

MAKING YOUR PARTNER SMILE

Pair with a partner. Stand opposite your partner and devote about twenty seconds to each of the tasks that follow. At the end of the list, change roles, and repeat the exercise.

1. Study your partner's eyebrows.

2. Make your partner smile.

3. Study your partner's mouth.

4. Make your partner laugh.

5. Ask yourself: What makes my partner laugh?
6. Make your partner laugh *loudly*.
7. Study your partner's eyes.
8. Ask yourself: What does my partner see, looking at me?
9. Make your partner take you seriously.
10. Smile.
11. Take your partner's two hands.
12. See the four-year-old child your partner once was.
13. See the corpse your partner eventually will be.
14. Make your partner smile.

When you make your partner smile, or laugh, or take you seriously, you are not merely "doing something"; you are doing something *to (or with) someone else.* That is, you are participating in an interaction. All acting is interacting with other persons.

Your acting partner is a person. He or she was an infant once and is as mortal as you are. Your acting partner (like you) is a sexual person, a fearful person, a caring person, and a person who has profound desires. In other words, your acting partner is not just "your acting partner." He or she is an individual and, potentially, a source of great inspiration for you.

The more fully you contact your acting partner, the more fully you will be acting. Acting is never something you can do by yourself because acting is person-to-person communication. In order to "live" onstage, you must first make the other characters, your acting partners, "live" in your mind. Your communication—your acting—will ultimately depend as much on them as on you, and on the intensity with which you make yourself believe in them and care about them.

Interactive Dynamics

The actor's awareness of others is not merely a matter of dispassionate observation. Stage relationships that are properly dramatic must suggest a potential for dramatic *change:* usually the potential for love, on the one hand, or the potential for physical or psychological violence. These potentials are the *dynamics* of relationships. Because this potential for love or violence is al-

ways present, we say that the actors are *vulnerable*. Exercise 2–2 is
a simple way of approaching actor-to-actor vulnerability.

EXERCISE 2–2

VULNERABILITY

Pair with a partner, and designate one of you to be "A" and the other
"B." Memorize and quickly "rehearse" this contentless scene. (A contentless scene is one in which the words, by themselves, do not clearly
reveal any specific characters or plot; it is a scene that has no specified dramatic content.)

A: One.

B: Two.

A: Three.

B: Four.

A: Five.

B: Six.

A: Seven.

B: Eight.

A: Nine!

B: Ten!

"Perform" the scene while imagining each of these situations:

1. You have reason to believe that your acting partner may be plan-
   ning to murder you and that he or she may have a concealed
   weapon.

2. You were separated from a beloved sibling when you were three
   years old, and you have reason to believe that your acting partner
   is that sibling.

3. Person "A" has reason to believe (1) above, and Person "B" has
   reason to believe (2).

4. Person "B" has reason to believe (1) above, and Person "A" has
   reason to believe (2).

Vulnerability, a crucial component of all acting, means that
you are *aware* of the other actor as a complete person, and that

you are also aware of *the potential good or harm that can come from the relationship* between you.

Interactive dynamics suggest that relationships are not merely static arrangements between agreeable people, but are evolving interplays of mutuality and independence, attraction and separation, desire and fear. The person you meet in the cafeteria today *could* be your life companion twenty years from now; the person you are rehearsing a scene with *could* pull out a revolver and shoot you. The normal human impulse is to ignore such remote potentials. The actor's impulse, in an acting situation, should be to make them vivid, to create the dynamics of the relationship wherever possible and appropriate. Even a scene as content-free as "one, two, three . . . ten" can become a vivid and exciting drama if you explore the potential for both love and violence that might be imagined as existing between characters "A" and "B" and the vulnerability of the actors to those potentials.

EXERCISE 2–3

DISCOVERY

Pair with a partner and designate an "A" and a "B." "Play" the following interchange. Try to discover as much as possible about your partner by studying his or her tone of voice, expression, and changes in breathing pattern, and by speculating on his or her possible thoughts or fantasies.

A: Can I see you on Monday?

B: How about Tuesday?

A: How about Wednesday?

B: How about Thursday?

A: How about Friday?

B: How about Saturday?

A: How about Sunday?

B: OK, then, Sunday.

Don't make any effort to give clever readings, and don't worry about your own delivery of the lines. Concentrate entirely on your partner and finding out what you can about him or her.

Try this alternate scene, too, with the same instructions:

A: I know you will.

B: I know I won't.

A: I know you will.

B: I know I won't.

A: I know you will.

B: I know I won't.

A: I know you will.

B: I know I won't.

The dialogs in this lesson were chosen because they can be memorized instantly. Memorized dialog from scenes that you work on later also can be used in this exercise, if you wish to return to it.

The Character

Here's an important question that may have occurred to you already: When you make your partner smile, or when you imagine your partner as a long-lost sibling, or when you ask your partner if he or she can see you on Sunday, is your partner a classmate, or an actor, or a character? Philosophers may answer that question in a variety of ways, but for you there is only one answer: *Your partner is always a character.* The moment an acting exercise begins, it exists within a theatrical context. At that point, all participants are characters, and all behavior is acting, or "playing."

This is a liberating answer. It means that the interactions between your partner and yourself take place within an overall context in which you have already agreed to "play," or to interact as characters. Therefore you can experience your feelings fully; you can experience the depth of love, lust, violence, and ambition within a dramatic context (even in an exercise or improvisation), without committing yourself in any personal ("outside of class") way. Indeed, you can explore the extremities—and profundities—of feelings within the "playing" arena and return to your more private personality when the exercise (or play, or improvisation) is over. The ability to see your classmates as characters—which extends to seeing your best friend as Iago and your worst enemy as Romeo—is the ability to free your feelings so as to act vividly and intensely with other people.

Tactics

Tactics are the strategies of human communication; they are the active ingredients of dynamic interactions. Most of the tactics of everyday life are simple and benign, generated more by spontaneous impulse than by conscious plan. Smiling, for example, encourages agreement and tolerance; raising the level of the voice, on the other hand, encourages compliance. Some tactics are used to seek the support of other characters; some to silence their opposition.

In the effort to achieve victories and overcome obstacles, the actor continually tries to put some pressure on the other actors—who are, of course, characters in the play or scene. This pressure is real; it may be the seductiveness of a raised eyebrow, the menace of a clenched fist, or the bedazzlement of a brilliantly articulated argument, but it is a pressure felt by the other actors and by the audience alike. Your power in playing tactics will determine your authority and magnetism on stage.

EXERCISE 2–4
USING TACTICS

Pair with a partner. Imagine that the nonsense word "Beetaratagang" means "Get out of here!" in some foreign language. Imagine that the nonsense word "Cleridipity" means "Come over here" in the same language. Take turns playing these situations:

1. Order your acting partner away by saying "Beetaratagang!" to him or her.

2. Urge your acting partner to come toward you by saying "Cleridipity" to him or her.

3. Send your partner away with "Beetaratagang" and then draw him or her back with "Cleridipity." Reverse.

To communicate with your partner, use body language, tone of voice, inflection, gesture, facial expression, threats of physical force, seductive and inductive postures—everything you can think of *except* physical contact.

Full contact with an acting partner depends on your willingness to engage in genuine emotional interaction with another person: to frighten, to encourage, to alarm, and to entertain your acting partner. The desire to achieve your victory, coupled with a willingness and ability to translate that desire into effective person-to-person behavior, creates the baseline of your acting performance. Your ability to make "Beetaratagang" so unsettling as to force someone to go away, or to make "Cleridipity" so evocative as to induce someone to approach you, is a primal acting ability, coming wholly from *you* and not from a text or a dramatic staging or interpretation.

EXERCISE 2–5

ONE TWO THREE FOUR FIVE SIX SEVEN

This exercise is intended to deepen your concentration and extend your repertoire of communication tactics. Trying is more important than succeeding in these tasks.

Without touching your partner, and using only the words "one two three four five six seven" on each task, try to elicit the following actions or feelings from your partner.

1. Make your partner sit down next to you.

2. Make your partner kneel before you.

3. Make your partner feel sorry for you.

4. Make your partner happy.

5. Make your partner nervous.

6. Make your partner aroused.

7. Make your partner feel chilled.

Summary

Acting is not something you do by yourself; invariably it is something you do to, with, and for at least one other person. Most of what the audience eventually sees in an acting performance is a *relationship* between characters—a relationship created by you and your acting partner. In order for that relationship to be a dramatic one, it must be dynamic. The actors must be vulnerable to one another. A potential for good or harm—preferably for both—must be clearly implied by the relationship, and the actors, through the use of interpersonal tactics, must put pressure on each other to change or improve their relationship.

Beginning to Act

Contentless Scene

In the preceding pages we have introduced several foundations of acting: victories, obstacles, vulnerability, projection, and the person-to-person contact and tactical interplay that characterize dynamic relationships. These fundamentals can all be explored in a series of contentless scenes—so called because they are devoid of fixed plot or characterizations.

A contentless scene can be memorized quite rapidly—usually within about ten minutes. In a group situation, actors should pair up and memorize their parts aloud, one person of each pair memorizing part "A," the other part "B." During memorization, no attempt should be made to create an interpretation with the lines, or to "fix" readings or inflections of individual lines; the lines are to be learned *simply by rote.*

When the scene has been memorized, the actors should then *switch partners,* so that each "A" will be paired with a "B" with whom they have not rehearsed or spoken this dialog. The contentless scenes may be "performed" many times, switching partners each time, so that each time the scene is produced, it is produced *without prior rehearsal* between the two paired actors.

EXERCISE 3–1

IMPROVISATION

Perform this scene without rehearsal or preplanning of any kind. For each performance, however, use one of the seven situations on the list below.

Scene: What did you do last night?

A: Hi!

B: Hello.

A: How's everything?

B: Fine. I guess.

A: Do you know what time it is?

B: No. Not exactly.

A: Don't you have a watch?

B: Not on me.

A: Well?

B: Well what?

A: What did you do last night?

B: What do you mean?

A: What did you do last night?

B: Nothing.

A: Nothing?

B: I said, nothing!

A: I'm sorry I asked.

B: That's all right.

The Seven Situations

1. "A" is a parent; "B" is a teenager. The scene takes place at the breakfast table; "B" eating a bowl of cereal, "A" entering.

2. "A" and "B" (different sexes) are a young married couple. Last night, after an argument, "B" left the apartment. It is now the following morning. "A" is washing dishes. "B" returns.

3. "A" and "B" (same sex) are roommates. Both have been involved with the same boy (or girl) during the past few weeks, both are still

interested in pursuing the relationship, both are somewhat suspicious of the other's secrecy. They meet while returning to their room after a night's absence.

4. "A" and "B" (different sexes) are classmates who have been romantically interested in each other for some time. They meet in a cafeteria by accident, and "A" sits down next to "B."

5. "A" and "B" (same sex) are auditioning for an important role. It is rumored that the director plays sexual favorites in casting. "A" and "B" meet at the bulletin board to await the announcement of callbacks.

6. "A" and "B" are siblings. "B" has recently been released from a psychiatric care clinic after a suicide attempt. After "B" has stayed out all night, "A" finds "B" in the waiting room of a bus depot.

7. "A" and "B" are friends. "B" has recently been released from a psychiatric care unit after maniacally attacking a friend with a butcher knife. "A," aware of this, comes upon "B" in an isolated spot.

When many variations on contentless scenes are performed, with the actors switching partners each time, several things become evident:

The content of the scene is created entirely by the given situation and the actors: The words become instruments of the action, not the dictator of plot, character, or behavior. Thus the acting becomes a way of creating a spontaneously changing relationship—and the plot develops entirely out of what happens between you and your acting partner.

The scene is happening in real time; that is, it is being *experienced* while it is being performed. One often talks, in acting, about "creating the illusion of the first time."* In Exercise 3–1 "the first time" is no illusion; you are indeed experiencing the interchange for the first time, live and unrehearsed.

You will find that there is nothing you can do in Exercise 3–1 to succeed "on your own." Whatever happens in the contentless scene depends not on you or on your acting partner, but on

---

*The notion, first expressed by nineteenth-century American actor-playwright William Gillette, that acting should appear unrehearsed, that each speech should be delivered as though the character was uttering the words "for the first time."

what happens between the two of you. Person-to-person contact, tactical interplay, projection, and vulnerability are demand-
ed by the exercise itself. In these situations, feelings come to
you naturally.

The scene is *unpredictable*. One of the problems in the theatre is
that scripts, by nature, are predictable: The last act has already
been written and rehearsed when the curtain rises on Act I. Exercise 3–1 helps you avoid—for a time at least—the problem of
making a predictable scene look unpredictable: The scene *is* unpredictable, and neither you nor your acting partner knows, at
the outset, how it is going to end. Such a condition keeps you
alert, involved, and mentally active throughout the scene, often
to an extraordinary degree.

Intensifiers

Exercise 3–1 can be repeated almost indefinitely, inasmuch as
there are hundreds of possible situations and thousands of implications that will make every rendition fresh and different. The
exercise can also be intensified by adding obstacles to the situations.

EXERCISE 3–2

INTENSIFYING

Replay the dialog in Exercise 3–1 using one of the seven situations,
plus one of the obstacles on the following list. Repeat the exercise by
varying both situations and obstacles.

1. Your acting partner has been known to carry a revolver.

2. You feel sick to your stomach.

3. The odor in the room is noxious.

4. You suspect your acting partner is dying.

5. Your acting partner is partly deaf.

6. It is very cold.

7. Your acting partner seems sexually frustrated.

8. Your acting partner seems especially flushed.

9. You do not feel that you can stand up without losing control of your bowels.

10. You feel that if you speak loudly, you will start crying.

The intensifiers are *not* things that you play, or that you have to show in any way. Indeed, they are actually obstacles that you will have to struggle *against*: against showing them, and against their standing in your way. The struggle against obstacles makes you perform more intensely; when speaking to a partly deaf person, for example, you must speak louder and with greater articulation. Obstacles cannot be so great that they inhibit action altogether (that is why we say a *partly* deaf person), or so insignificant that you can forget about them entirely. They must be bold enough to make you work harder, and difficult enough to make your quest dramatically interesting.

Physicalizers

Sometimes extraordinary changes occur in scenes simply when the locale is changed, or when the actors are asked to carry on some sort of underlying action, such as jogging. Physicalizing a scene frequently brings out subtler undertones and more poignant transitions; it also gets the acting "into the body" more than simply sitting and talking.

EXERCISE 3–3
VARYING LOCALE OR ACTION

Replay the contentless scene in any of these physicalized variations:

1. While jogging
2. While setting the table together
3. While lying down at the beach
4. "B" lying in bed, "A" seated at foot of bed
5. While playing basketball
6. While arm wrestling
7. While dancing to music

8. While doing pushups
9. While eating a real banana
10. While giving a backrub, one to the other

Invent your own variations!

EXERCISE 3–4
VARYING THE DIALOG

Memorize the following dialog. Then, using the new dialog, repeat
Exercises 3–1, 3–2, and 3–3.

SCENE: "I'M GOING AWAY."

A: Hi!

B: Hello.

A: You all right?

B: Yes.

A: Are you sure?

B: Yes, I'm sure. A little headache, that's all.

A: Oh, good. You want some aspirin?

B: No. Don't be so helpful, OK?

A: You are upset.

B: Good Lord!

A: OK, OK. I thought you might want to talk.

B: About what?

A: About anything.

B: I'm going away.

A: What do you mean?

B: I'm going away, that's all.

A: Where?

B: Not far. Don't get excited.

A: When?

B: Now. *(Starts to leave)*

The situations in the previous scene will work here, but you can invent dozens of other situations as well.

Summary

The contentless scene—in which the dialog is essentially ambiguous, trivial, or both—provides an opportunity to explore the playing of victories, tactics, and relationships in a fresh, improvisatory manner, without preplanning or rehearsing. The personal interaction can be intensified by establishing obstacles to the basic victories. Physicalizing the scenes may bring out subtle meanings and pointed "moments" that are valuable in an acting performance.

Tactics

Punishment and Reward

Most of us would like to believe that we don't use tactics in our everyday lives, that we simply "live and let live" without trying to manipulate our friends and acquaintances. But as we saw in Lesson 2, this is not the case. When someone is talking to us, we smile to invite more talking or look skeptical to shut the fellow up. We frown at a disobedient child and raise our voices to make sure our instructions are followed. Or we squat humbly at the feet of a celebrated guru and beam upward to indicate the respect that may draw forth a word of wisdom. These are inter-personal tactics, and we use them whenever we are in the presence of others.

Dogs, cats, and two-month-old babies use tactics too; any thinking species with needs and wants uses tactics to seek and achieve its moment-to-moment goals and victories. Acting, which is interacting, requires that the actor learn how to play tactics: forcefully, winsomely, and engagingly.

There are basically two kinds of tactics: those that threaten and those that induce—punishment and reward, in other words. Tactics that threaten say, "Do what I want or I'll make your life miserable." Tactics that induce say, "Do what I want and you'll be happier for it." Raising your voice is a threatening tactic, smiling an inductive tactic; both are common in everyday life and on the stage that mirrors life.

Playing Tactics

When you play tactics on stage, you *really* play them. When your character is trying to threaten another character, you try to threaten your acting partner. On the other hand, if your character is trying to encourage warmth from another character, you make every effort to induce that warmth from the actor who is your partner.

But remember this ground rule: The actor must never physically hurt or sexually abuse another actor during an exercise, scene, or improvisation. Any acting involving physical force, combat, or overt sexual behavior must be rehearsed and talked through until both actors are fully comfortable with it. It is often useful to have a general understanding of what constitutes "sexual abuse" in an exercise situation, as this definition may vary depending on the age, experience, and cultural milieu of the actors involved.

EXERCISE 4–1

FRIGHTEN YOUR PARTNER

Pair with a partner. Using one of the phrases below, try to *actually frighten* your partner.

1. Shut up!
2. Get out of here!
3. Leave me alone!
4. Go to hell!
5. Go on, kill me!

EXERCISE 4–2

BUILDING INTENSITY

Using the phrases in Exercise 4–1, again trying to frighten your partner, repeat each phrase three times, improvising "improvements" to build the intensity. Example: "Shut up! Shut up, damn it! Shut up before you get hurt!" Use only mild profanity—or none. Try to increase your intensity by nonverbal means: the power of your voice, the cutting edge of your inflection, the command of your physical presence, the *implied* threat of your gesture and expression, and the clear sign of authority denoted by the strength of your emotional commitment.

EXERCISE 4–3
MAKE YOUR PARTNER CRY

Repeat Exercise 4–2 several times, switching roles between you and your partner, and concentrate on trying to make your partner come to tears. This victory gives the tactic a physiological reality, and gives you something to look for and struggle to achieve. *It is not necessary to achieve this victory; it is only necessary that you try.* Plays are filled with characters who fail to achieve their victories; the actors need only play their efforts—their *genuine* efforts.

Trying to make the other actor cry is one of the strongest victories an actor can seek, inasmuch as it brings to the surface thoughts and emotions, often repressed from childhood, that unlock a great deal of subconscious behavior. Our earliest tears stem from pain, rage, and fright—often the fright induced by a seemingly omnipotent parent—and any improvisation or dialog that brings back those primal situations can be an immensely stimulating acting discovery. Trying to make somebody cry brings out qualities of behavior that are rarely seen in the classroom, and liberates much of the inherent power of the performer.

EXERCISE 4–4
MOVEMENT AND CONTACT

Repeat Exercise 4–3 several times, adding physical gestures and movements that intensify the pursuit of your victory. Use *agreed-upon* physical contact: a soft shove on your partner's shoulder or shoulders; seizing your partner's wrist; or slapping your partner's arms and torso. Be sure to use the physical business simply as a means of adding force and emphasis to your lines—not as a way of making your partner cry by inflicting real pain. The threatening tactics of an actor are psychological only; physical violence, on stage, is *always* simulated.

You will quickly tire of threatening or frightening exercises, which can be sustained only for a very short time in any event. Ordinarily they should be alternated with inductive exercises.

EXERCISE 4–5

ENCOURAGE YOUR PARTNER

Pair with a partner. Using one of the phrases below, try to encourage your partner to come closer to you, to sit down, or to engage in behavior that you suggest would be enjoyable:

1. Come on over here.
2. Sit down next to me.
3. I want to talk with you.
4. I have something I think you'd like.
5. Please.
6. (Make something up yourself.)

Repeat Exercise 4–5, building on your original phrase with improvised elaborations. Use your body, your intonation and inflection, the sound of your voice, and manner of your gesture and expression to induce calm, trust, and amusement in your acting partner. Work to make your partner *smile* or *laugh*. As a physicalizer, take one or both of your partner's hands in yours. Try to coax your partner into a genuine rapport with your desires.

Induction tactics (which tend to "induce" behavior rather than threaten noncompliance) are the common stuff of everyday human intercourse, much more common than threats both in life and on the stage. When well played, they give an actor magnetism and charm, just as threatening tactics, when well played, lend an actor a commanding forcefulness.

Both threatening and inductive tactics are efforts on your part to influence the behavior and ideas of the other actor; to interfere with the other actor's state of tranquillity or direction. By playing tactics, the actor creates a character who is trying to shape the scene, the only kind of character that is dramatically interesting. Characters in plays are never merely observers. Even those characters who describe themselves as observers, such as the title character in *I Am a Camera*, are active in interpersonal engagements. Characters in plays are all interpersonally active: They are always trying to influence, to overthrow, to impress, to seduce, to win over, to suppress, to engage somebody. This is why tactics are so important to the actor: They are the actual "happenings" onstage; they are what is going on between the characters—and therefore between the actors.

Alternating Tactics

Tactics are almost never monolithic on stage; most of the time they alternate—often with mercurial speed—between threats and inducements. Actors who can switch between hair-raising forcefulness and ingratiating charm in an instant—actors such as Laurence Olivier, for example—are widely admired for encompassing this range of interpersonal effectiveness, which is dramatically thrilling because it suggests an almost explosive unpredictability.

EXERCISE 4–6

MIXING TACTICS

Pair with a partner. Using the phrases in Exercises 4–1 and 4–5 (or similar phrases), create a sequence of tactical approaches to your partner that alternate from threatening to inductive to threatening; or inductive to threatening to inductive. For example:

1. Get out of here! I said get out of here! Will you get out of here! Come here. Come on over here. Please? Shut up! Shut up, John! I said shut up!

2. Ellen, come up here. Come on, sit down. I want to talk to you. Will you take off your shoe? Take off your shoe, Ellen! I said, take off your shoe! Please? You'll be happier, I promise. Come on.

The Middle Ranges

Making someone cry and making someone laugh are at the extreme ends of tactical behavior; in the middle there is making somebody listen, making somebody care, making somebody proud, or worried, or happy, or agreeable. These are the middle ranges of acting, and this is where most of an actor's time is spent.

EXERCISE 4–7
ELIMINATING THE EXTREMES

Pair with a partner, and designate one of you as "A," the other as "B." Memorize and "play" the following scene, escalating steadily from inductive tactics at the beginning to threatening ones at the end:

1. A: I know you will.

   B: No, I won't.

2. A: I know you will.

   B: No, I won't.

3. A: I know you will.

   B: No, I won't!

4. A: I know you will!

   B: No, I won't!

5. A: *(Pulling out all the stops)* I know you will!!

   B: *(Ditto)* No, I won't!!

Repeat several times, each time intensifying the escalation by adding facial expression, gesture, and whole body movements.

Now, with the pattern of five exchanges fairly set in your mind, repeat but do not escalate the last (fifth) exchange; in other words, hold the last exchange down to the level of the fourth.

Do the scene again, holding the last two exchanges down to the level of the third.

The first and fifth exchanges in Exercise 4–7 are the extremities; the second, third, and fourth are the middle ranges where most acting occurs. The extremities must always be there, in the actor's mind at least, for they define what's finally at stake in a scene or play. But most acting exchanges take place at the level of forceful—but not extreme—tactical interaction. Working on the middle levels, and on the continuum from powerful induction to electrifying threats, actors explore and develop their tactical range.

The exercises in this lesson should be considered "études," or studies, that allow you to explore a mere fraction of acting, but an important fraction: those moments, usually at the climax of a scene, which require you to be deeply committed to succeeding in some cause or other—and trying to succeed by influencing the feelings and behavior of your acting partner. When these "études" are put into a play, with all your power at their service, they become the key moments in your performance.

Summary

There are two basic types of tactics; those that threaten and those that induce. A successful actor learns how to play both types strongly and in rapid alternation. There is also a broad middle range of tactics between the extremities, which are in process most of the time—although the extremities are always latent in the actor's mind. Tactics are *real* interpersonal behaviors, designed to influence other people; they should be played on stage as intensely as in real life, and should aim at creating real reactions (including physiological reactions) in the other actors. Playing tactics forcefully, intensely, and physically brings to the surface human emotions—both from you and from your acting partner—and creates vivid and dynamic acting relationships.

Expectations

Expecting Victory

Expectation is at the leading edge of an actor's performance; the character must not only *try* to achieve a victory, he or she must *expect* to achieve it. This expectation may be irrational—but that is the character's irrationality, not the actor's. You have read the script beforehand, but your character has not; therefore your character can expect victory even if victory is not going to be the end result.

Thus when trying to make your acting partner cry, you must *expect* your partner to cry; that is, you must expect that if you try as hard as you can, you will emerge victorious. This expectation creates the energy of performance—and pulls energy out of you that you could not otherwise "push" simply by trying to be "energetic."

Expectation gives rise to several "E" words: *energy, excitement, electricity,* and *enthusiasm,* all of which characterize the high-voltage performances that have the capacity to stimulate an audience. Audience empathy, in fact, comes almost entirely from the audience's identification with the character's *expectations.* This is surprising at first glance. We tend to think that audiences identify with a character's suffering, and beginning actors often play self-pity in the mistaken notion that this will stimulate a sympathetic audience reaction. But the audience can identify only with a character's expectations and enthusiasms. The excitement of a deaf and blind Helen Keller's learning to understand the word *water*, for example, creates the tremendous emotional response to William Gibson's fine play, *The Miracle Worker*; it is *not* our pity for Keller's handicap that generates this feeling. Character expectations carry the audience along, pulling them into the action and sweeping them up into the emotions of the play. A character's *enthusiasms* are the points of audience contact; they determine the elation we feel when the character succeeds, and the poignancy we share when the character fails. Expectation provides the context of the character's behavior for the audience, and the impulse for the behavior for the actor who plays it; enthusiasm, which is itself theatrically compelling, provides the excitement of dramatic conflict.

Conversely, a character who is resolutely unenthusiastic— who has no expectations of success—is relegated to a purely functional role in the drama and will inevitably appear to be "uninvolved" no matter how sensitively and carefully the role is otherwise performed. Audiences cannot—or will not—identify with predetermined "losers," nor do they often find such people believable as realistic characters. For the fact is that virtually everybody sets out on difficult courses with at least some expectation of success (even an irrational expectation), and that expectation makes people, including dramatic characters, interesting—and sometimes heroic.

EXERCISE 5–1

PLAYING BORED

Memorize the following line: "I am bored, bored, bored." This is Masha's famous line in Chekhov's *The Three Sisters,* loosely translated. The situation: Masha, the eldest of the sisters, is one of several at a gathering of family and friends in a small provincial town. She is speaking to no one in particular—or to everyone in general.

Now "play" the line to your class.

How did you play the line in Exercise 5–1?

Did you try to "act bored"? To convey boredom, to demonstrate what it's like to be bored, to imitate what you would consider the attitude of a bored person? That would be wrong, as it would ignore the fundamental principles we have been talking about, and to substitute some sort of "demonstration" for the dynamic interplay of victories, obstacles, tactics, and expectations.

What is Masha's victory? Probably to get *un*bored: to stimulate someone to entertain her (or to fall in love with her—which is what happens). Perhaps Masha wants to call attention to herself, or to make a joke out of her boredom, or to parody the decadence of her society (to parody the kind of characters one finds in Chekhov!), or to liven up the party.

Positive Objectives

There are hundreds of possible interpretations of the line "I am bored, bored, bored"; but the best ones all lead to Masha's effort to do something positive, to stimulate something desirable. If she is bored (and who knows—perhaps she isn't telling the whole truth!), her reason for saying she's bored is not to admit that fact but to change it—to act upon her environment rather than give in to it. We speak only in order to change things, to improve things, not simply to confirm reality. We are under no obligation to speak at all; if we do speak, it is to have some impact on our world and on the people that surround us.

So, what is Masha's expectation? Experiment with any of these five possibilities, and then play her line again to real or imaginary guests in your/her house:

1. You want to liven up the party.
2. You want _____ to fall in love with you.
3. You want your sisters to acknowledge your intellectual superiority.
4. You want everyone to laugh.
5. You want to make fun of _____.

EXERCISE 5–2

ENTHUSIASM

The following speeches lend themselves to the exploration of positive expectations and enthusiasms—sometimes obviously and sometimes only after a bit of searching. Memorize each short speech, find a positive victory to seek, and imagine some quite wonderful result that you can enthusiastically expect to occur. Say the line, to either a real or an imaginary person or persons.

1. "Oh heavens, how I long for a little ordinary human enthusiasm— that's all. I want to hear a warm thrilling voice cry out 'Hallelujah! Hallelujah! I'm alive!' I've an idea. Why don't we have a little game? Let's pretend that we're human beings, and that we're actually alive. Just for a little while. What do you say?" (Jimmy Porter, in John Osborne's *Look Back in Anger*).

2. "Use your head, can't you, use your head, you're on earth, there's no cure for that!" (Hamm, in Samuel Beckett's *Endgame*).

3. "I'll put up with any torture you impose. Anything, anything would be better than this agony of mind, this creeping pain that gnaws and fumbles and caresses one and never hurts quite enough." (Garcin, in Jean-Paul Sartre's *No Exit*).

4. "I don't want realism. I want magic. I don't tell the truth. I tell what ought to be truth. And if that is sinful, then let me be damned for it!" (Blanche, in Tennessee Williams' *A Streetcar Named Desire*).

5. "I'm not a leader of men, Willy, and neither are you. You were never anything but a hard-working drummer who landed in the ash can like all the rest of them. I'm one dollar an hour, Willy! I tried seven states and couldn't raise it. A buck an hour! Do you gather my meaning? I'm not bringing home any prizes any more, and you're going to stop waiting for me to bring them home!" (Biff, in Arthur Miller's *Death of a Salesman*).

6. "You've finally got the game of life licked, don't you see that? Then why the hell don't you get pie-eyed and celebrate? Why don't you laugh and sing Sweet Adeline? The only reason I can think of is, you're putting on this rotten half-dead act just to get back at me! Because you hate my guts!" (Hickey, in Eugene O'Neill's *The Iceman Cometh*).

7. "Oh, did you believe my courage would never come back? did you believe that I was a deserter? that I, who have stood in the streets and taken my people to heart, and talked of the holiest and greatest things with them, could ever turn back and chatter foolishly about nothing in a drawing room? Never, never, never, never: Major Barbara will die with the colors. Glory, Hallelujah!" (Major Barbara, in George Bernard Shaw's *Major Barbara*).

8. "It's three hours since you've met and known and loved each other. Kiss each other quickly. Look at him. He hesitates. He trembles. Happiness frightens him . . . How like a man! O, Irma, kiss him, kiss him! If two people who love each other let a single instant wedge itself between them, it grows—it becomes a month, a year, a century; it becomes too late! Kiss him, Irma, kiss him while there is still time, or in a moment his hair will be white and there will be another madwoman in Paris." (The Madwoman, in Jean Giraudoux's *The Madwoman of Chaillot*).

9. "My ears have yet not drunk a hundred words
   Of thy tongue's uttering, yet I know the sound;
   Art thou not Romeo, and a Montague?"

   (Juliet, in William Shakespeare's *Romeo and Juliet*)

10. "So, gentleman,
    With all my love I do commend me to you:
    And what so poor a man as Hamlet is
    May do, to express his love and friending to you,
    God willing, shall not lack. Let us go in together;
    And still your fingers on your lips, I pray.
    The time is out of joint: O cursed spite,
    That ever I was born to set it right!
    Nay, come, let's go together."

    (Hamlet, in William Shakespeare's *Hamlet*)

Learning to play speeches positively, with expectations of some concrete and specific victory in mind, is a strong step away from grievous actor problems—most particularly self-consciousness and a tendency to play toward self-pity, empty sarcasm, sentimentality, and pious moralizing. No action can be convincing on stage—and no actor can be sufficiently confident in his or her role—without an expectation of success in the action's outcome. Creating that expectation—which the script does not always confirm at the play's conclusion—is the actor's job, and often the actor's most delicate job.

EXERCISE 5–3

TRY THE IMPOSSIBLE

Try to jump twenty feet in the air. (That's right, you can't do it. But try.) Now try to jump twenty feet in the air, expecting to succeed! Think of the prizes you are going to win! Think of the cheering crowds! The adulation! The rewards! The romantic opportunities! You can do it! Do it again! Again! AGAIN!!

What happens in this progressive escalation of expectation in Exercise 5–3? Did the expectation of victory (even of an impossible victory) give you a greater tone, strength, and vivacity? Did you jump even higher? Did you enjoy the exercise more? Did you get more of your body into play? More of your emotions? Were you less self-conscious?

Chances are that you answered "yes" to all those questions. Positive expectation and enthusiasm have brought far more out of you than merely following a stage direction. It was your *imagination* that made you jump higher, act more energetically, feel more deeply, and perform more vividly. And the same process is at work in a subtle and complex performance of a dramatic role.

EXERCISE 5–4

TACTICS AND EXPECTATIONS

Go back to the exercises in Lesson 4 and repeat them with *escalating expectations* of victory.

Summary

Positive expectation, on the actor's part, lends his or her portrayal a necessary excitement and energy. Not all characters succeed, of course, but they must be shown to expect success and even to be enthusiastic about their prospects, if their actions are to excite audience interest and empathy. Even the most despairing of dramatic characters must have this quality of positive expectation, for it is only when their expectations are dashed that their pathos can be shared.

VOTE

A Basic Method

The foundations of an actor's approach have been set out in the previous lessons; admittedly, there's a good deal to keep in mind at one time.

VOTE is an easy-to-remember acronym that stands for and brings together the four basic principles. VOTE, therefore, represents a basic method for approaching an acting assignment. The letters individually stand for

Victory

Other

Tactics

Expectation

Let us go over these terms with an eye to their interdependence and mutual relationship.

Victory is the actor's goal, which elsewhere has been called the actor's objective, intention, or purpose. Any of these words will suffice, but *victory*, with its exciting associations, is more emotionally vivid than the more clinical synonyms. Everything you do on stage must be in the quest for some victory. Moreover, that victory should be something quite specific and outgoing: not just "I want to find self-fulfillment," but "I want to be King of Denmark" or "I want to marry Romeo."

The *other* is the person (or persons) with whom, for whom, or from whom you seek your victory. There is *always* an other in acting; no victory can be achieved simply by yourself. Thus Hamlet cannot simply say, "I want to be King of Denmark," and have a crown appear above his head; nor can Juliet say, "I want to be happily married," and then happily marry. Not in good theatre, anyway. In drama, all the victories must be hard-earned and must be earned through interpersonal struggle. There are simply no good plays about characters learning the multiplication table or developing a personal philosophy without an interpersonal struggle.

The other in a scene, therefore, is what makes victories difficult; often the other is your chief obstacle. In acting, victories worth seeking must be achievable only with the compliance, complicity, or defeat of other characters. To the extent that the obstacles posed by others are formidable, your character can be seen as heroic. To the extent that the other characters are complex, your character can be profound. The nature of your actions —and of your acting—will be determined by your confrontation with the other who stands between you and victory.

Putting together the confrontation of victory and other, you will ask of a given scene or exercise:

1. What is my victory?
2. How will the other(s) affect my gaining it?
    a. How can they help?
    b. How may they hurt?
3. How must I affect the other(s)?
4. What are my best tactics?

Tactics are the character's means of trying to achieve victory; they are what gives acting its "guts."

Tactics—and trying to achieve victories through them—make acting "real" for the actors, and make actors indistinguishable from characters, at least from the audience's point of view. That is to say: Jane trying to get Jim to fall in love with her is absolutely indistinguishable from Juliet trying to get Romeo to fall in love with her, when Jane is playing Juliet and Jim is playing

Romeo. The lines are Shakespeare's, but the tactics are your own; tactics will come out of your life experience, not out of the script.

As we saw in Lesson 4, tactics can be divided between those that threaten and those that induce; they can be divided also into extreme tactics and a broad "middle range" of subtler tactics. A good actor will be able to move fluidly and purposefully from tactic to tactic in pursuit of victory. Tactical strength and tactical versatility are what make acting, by turns, forceful, seductive, visceral, and dramatic. Actors work all their lives on expanding and developing their tactical range.

Expectation, the last word on the list, gives tone, spring, and excitement to the dramatic quest for victory. It also lends every dramatic action at least a touch of enthusiasm, which can prove deliciously infectious. Too often actors choose to play for victories in an academic way, as perhaps may be implied by the overly clinical word *objective*. It is not that your character just "wants" something; people have all sorts of petty wants that are rarely worth dramatizing. Look at any fine play, and the chances are that the author was thinking of characters who not only "wanted" their victories, they *craved* them: They were *excited* and *enthusiastic* about them; deep in their hearts they were even sure (often mistakenly) that they were going to get them! *Expectation, excitement, enthusiasm,* and even *energy* are "E" words that make a memory package: They define characters who have not only wants, but passions! You are playing one of those characters. The victory you seek is not just an ordinary whim; it is the prime goal of your life, and it is within your reach if you try hard enough. Go for it! NOW!

"Getting Out the VOTE"

These "first six lessons"* have outlined a method of approaching any role. Approaching the role does not necessarily mean performing the role to everybody's satisfaction—much less to the demands of this highly regarded art—but it is the starting

---

The First Six Lessons is the subtitle of Richard Boleslavski's justly famous book, *Acting* (New York: Theatre Arts Books, 1933).

point for professional and beginner alike. Before a role may be played, it must be approached: It must be understood and created in *acting* terms. What makes the character not just an invention of the playwright, but a living, breathing, feeling, caring, *acting* person? Characters act. In order to play a character, you must play the character's actions—and in order to play that character brilliantly, you must create those actions in vivid detail and with believable intensity.

Getting out the VOTE, which means creating those actions in the context of victories, obstacles, tactics, and expectations, is the key to putting yourself into the role, and to approaching the character with the full resources of your acting instrument (your voice and body) and your personal history, intelligence, and emotional resourcefulness.

How do you get out the VOTE? Studying the script is, of course, the first step. But using your imagination is the more important second step—more important in that most of the "answers" aren't answers at all, but creations. For most of the VOTE aspects are only *implied* by the script—and determining which implications are the correct ones is a highly subjective and imaginative task. Study gives the main lines of a character's desires, but imagination fleshes them out. Indeed, that is one of the particular characteristics of drama, which, unlike narrative fiction, creates action only through spoken words and physical movement, not through thought revelations or extended third-person descriptions, except in rare cases.

Often the play is silent about matters crucial to the character. What does Hamlet really want from Ophelia? What are Cordelia's feelings and desires toward King Lear? The actor's *choices* —governed but not restricted by the actor's research—will determine the character's behavior.

EXERCISE 6–1:

THE VOTESHEET

The VOTEsheet is a starting point for analyzing any role. Using your imagination, take a blank piece of paper and answer the following questions about a dramatic character from a play you know. Reread the play first, with the questions in mind, and answer *as the character would:*

1. Basic information about the character

   Name:

   Sex:

   Age:

   Marital status and history:

   Educational level:

   Economic/social status:

2. Victory: What do I really want? When do I want it?

3. Other: From whom (in the play) do I want it? Who in the play can help me? Who in the play can hurt me? What are my deepest fears?

4. Tactics: How can I get it? How (and whom) can I threaten? How (and whom) can I induce?

5. Expectation: Why do I expect to get it? Why does it excite me? What will I do when I get it?

You may answer impressionistically or in lists, but answer vividly, not academically.

Now, memorize, rehearse, and play a scene, trying to implement your answers to these VOTEsheet questions.

Summary

VOTE is an acronym for Victory, Other, Tactics, and Expectation; in combination, these are the four coordinates of the actor's approach to any role. The VOTEsheet is the actor's basic list of questions, whose answers will create the foundation for approaching a specific character.

THE ACTOR'S TASKS

Part Two suggests practical methods for preparing an acting role for presentation, either in a scene for class or in a play. Naturally your instructor (in a class) or director (in a play) will provide some specific policies, advice, and guidance in your work; nonetheless it is finally up to you to develop a fundamental working method for preparing a role on your own.

Scenes are the basic medium of acting. The two-person scene, from three to eight minutes in length, drawn from any play (or adapted from other sources) is the basic exercise for the acting student. It involves, in microcosm, virtually all the acting skills a play involves, and yet can be prepared in a relatively short time with little or no cost.

This section deals primarily with scenes to be presented in class, although some discussion is devoted to scenes in plays, where the method may be somewhat different.

Memorizing

Choosing a Role

"How did you memorize all those lines?" is the first-time playgoer's oddly inappropriate remark at a backstage visit. Memorizing is simply the first of the actor's many practical duties in preparing and presenting a role to the public or to the class.

Memorizing is "donkey work," according to Alec McGowan, who once memorized the Gospel According to Saint Mark for a spectacularly successful one-man presentation. But if pursued diligently and immediately, this donkey work goes hand-in-glove with the actor's understanding of the role so as to provide the firmest possible basis for richly experimental and emotionally charged acting.

Before memorization, of course, the role must be chosen and the script prepared. In a play, both these functions are largely taken care of by the director. In a class presentation, you are usually asked to select a scene yourself, and sometimes a partner as well. Every class and every instructor has certain rules and limits as to what sorts of scenes you should choose. In general, however, and absent instructions to the contrary, you should:

1. Choose roles of your own sex and close to your own age.

2. Choose roles in which you can clearly see something at stake, emotionally, for the character you will be playing.

3. Choose roles in which *something is happening in the scene itself*—as opposed to roles in which characters are talking about something that has already happened.
4. Choose roles in which you can identify with the character's struggle or dilemma.
5. Choose roles in which the characters and situation interest you *personally*.

You should also try to choose roles in scenes set in periods and styles that you understand well, and characters whose backgrounds you can identify with. And, given the opportunity, you should try to select scene partners of both sexes over the course of several scene assignments.

Editing a Scene

Sometimes it is necessary to edit a scene, to cut it down in length, or to combine two short scenes into a longer one, or to delete references within the scene that are out of context with the immediate matters at hand. Sometimes a little rewriting, if permitted by the instructor, may be useful for "writing out" a minor character in the scene.

Sometimes you can adapt a scene from a novel or short story by transcribing the dialog and omitting the narrative. Some outstanding, contemporary, realistic scenes for young people can be obtained this way, inasmuch as there are many more published novels than plays in any given year, and novels today tend to include extensive dialog. In adapting a novel for classroom scene use, you might consider yourself a practicing screenplay adaptor, for this is how many films begin.

Once a script in fully edited, you and your partner must obtain exact duplicate copies. You should also agree on the context of the scene: What is the basic relationship of the characters—as they both understand it to be—and what is happening in the scene as both characters understand it? These basic understandings should be just that—basic—one or two sentences that define only the outer boundaries of the scene. For example, " 'A' and 'B' are husband and wife. 'A' is trying to get 'B' to confess her adultery; 'B' is trying to make 'A' get dressed to go to a party."

You and your partner should read the scene once or twice together. Then memorization should commence.

Memorization Methods

Memorization is sometimes a difficult task; you should know that it invariably gets more difficult as you get older. Young children memorize almost immediately; two or three times through a script, and eight-year-olds will have their parts memorized; two or three more times through and they will have everybody else's parts memorized as well. Conversely, older actors frequently find memorization an absolute horror; many, indeed, give up the theatre for film and TV where they can use cue cards in lieu of memorizing and can (to a certain extent) demand retakes if they "dry up" (forget their lines).

You must learn your lines exactly, even for a simple scene performed in class. There are several reasons for this. First, that's the only way your partner can be secure about coming in on cue. Second, learning your lines exactly gives you a confidence in your role that you can never have if you're fishing for the exact way to say something. Third, such rewriting as you do when you paraphrase your lines invariably weakens your role; you will tend to reduce your role to a commonplace character, rather than rise to the level created by the author's words. Fourth, by paraphrasing you will probably defeat the author's sense of timing and diminish the power of the play's builds, climaxes, and rhythmic effects. Fifth, you will look bad in the eyes of those who know the play, and who will feel you haven't come up to the level of the character even if they are unaware of the specific line changes you have made. The slightest paraphrases of Shakespeare, for example, will make the acting seem profoundly "off" even if the source of the deviation is not apparent. And finally, you are simply insulting the author and the theatre itself by your laziness! So learn the lines exactly and by rote.

Many actors prefer to learn their lines in rehearsal, going through their parts "on book" (with script in hand) until the lines are embedded in their memory. This common practice invites certain problems. While going through a part on book, you are not acting; you are reacting to the book, not to the situation, and your main contact is not with the actors but with the script. You may well pick up patterns and readings in this "running through" that have nothing to do with the interactions between you and your partner, but rather with your immediate idea of what is "theatrical" about your part.

Try sitting down and memorizing your part first. By doing so, you will also be studying your part from your own character's point of view, not jumping to conclusions about what is the most theatrical way to play the scene. You can also develop your VOTEsheet as you memorize, studying the part while you are learning it.

Begin by underlining all your lines.

Start reading the text; read aloud for your own part, to yourself for the other character's part. Start with a quarter page or so, and go back to the beginning each time you complete this small section. Soon you will have your first few lines in your memory. Get a postcard or index card, and cover your first line. Read (to yourself) the line before it (your cue line), and recite your line from memory. Move the card down and read (to yourself) the next cue line or lines. Recite your next line from memory. Gradually go through the script, an hour or so at a time, lowering the card as you memorize more and more lines; eventually, you will have the text committed to memory.

At this point your memorization is still shallow; it needs to be set. Lines learned through study have a way of disappearing in the intensity of rehearsal; it is usually necessary to set them in a variety of ways. Record the cue lines on a tape recorder, and run your lines with the machine. Or get a friend to run lines with you. Run your lines aloud while driving, cycling, jogging, or showering. Run your lines with your acting partner, without trying to rehearse the actual staging. Write your lines out, by memory, in longhand or at the typewriter.

Cues

Always learn your lines with your partner's cues. There are usually two cues for each line: the action cue and the line cue. The action cue is what prompts you to speak; the line cue is the actual line you come in on. For example:

EDDIE: You gonna marry him?

CATHARINE: I don't know. We just been . . . goin' around, that's all. What've you got against him, Eddie? Please, tell me. What?

EDDIE: He don't respect you.

(Arthur Miller, *A View from the Bridge*)

The action cue for Eddie's last line here is "What've you got against him?" The line cue is "What?" Eddie's line is prepared in response to the action cue; it is held until the line cue.

Sometimes there are certain lines that seem to stick; an actor has memorized the part but one or two lines don't seem to come when cued. In this case the actor should study the cue (both action cue and line cue) and look for the precise linkage in the character's mind that triggers the response. Some linkages are obvious and rarely cause problems:

KRISTIN: Government rations are small but sure, and there's a pension for the widow and children.

JEAN: That's all very fine, but it's not in my line to start thinking at once about dying for my wife and children. I must say I had rather bigger ideas.

KRISTIN: You and your ideas! You've got obligations too, and you'd better start thinking about them.

JEAN: Don't *you* start pestering me about obligations.

(August Strindberg, *Miss Julie*)

This dialog is easy to memorize, for the action cues contain the germinal words of the responses. The following dialog is more difficult to memorize:

NICK: Everybody drinks a lot here in the East. Everybody drinks a lot in the Middle West, too.

GEORGE: We drink a great deal in this country, and I suspect we'll be drinking a great deal more, too . . . if we survive. We should be Arabs or Italians . . . the Arabs don't drink, and the Italians don't get drunk much, except on religious holidays. We should live on Crete, or something.

NICK: And that, of course, would make us cretins.

GEORGE: So it would. Tell me about your wife's money.

(Edward Albee, *Who's Afraid of Virginia Woolf?*)

This is caustic dialog, representing the half-clever repartee of heavy-drinking faculty colleagues at a late night party. It is difficult to memorize because it contains elliptical phrases, artificial constructions, and apparent non sequiturs, or illogical jumps. But there are some tricks to help you learn George's part, which is the particularly difficult one here.

George's analysis of the drinking habits of Arabs, Italians, and Cretans may be made simpler by picturing, in your head, a map of the Mediterranean, since all of these cultures bound this sea, and since George, a history professor, would be thinking of specific locales when he speaks; thus the line has more continuity than may be perceived at first glance. And George's apparent out-of-nowhere leap to "Tell me about your wife's money" may be memorized by associating Nick's "that would make us cretins" remark with the fleeting thought "anybody who would crack a joke like that must be a member of the idle rich." Or simpler yet, the transition may be memorized by picturing a cretin counting out money, an image that henceforth will be triggered by hearing Nick's "cretin" line, and will in turn trigger George's "money" line.

Studying the Part

Learning the lines of a role will teach you a great deal about the part that is not immediately apparent. Mainly, it will make clear to you the *logic* of your character's position, and how the lines develop not out of an author's whim, but out of a character's thinking process. Learning a long speech—out of George Bernard Shaw, for example, where the speeches can go on for pages —seems at first a formidable task, but as you start to work on it, the structure of the speech begins to assert itself in your mind. By learning the speech you begin to understand the speaker, and to understand why the words are in their particular order, and how the lines of thought, or argument, or reaction, develop in the character's mind. You may be amazed with the speed with which you can learn a long, well-crafted speech and the speed and conviction with which you can deliver it within a short period of time.

While you are memorizing your part, you begin to study it. What are your character's victories? How will other people—particularly the other person or persons in the scene(s) with you—help you to achieve that victory? How are they your obstacles? What sort of tactics can your character use? What sort did he or she grow up with? What is he or she afraid of? Excited by? How vivid are his or her expectations? How wild are his or her fantasies? How can you find the expectations of the character? The *enthusiasm?* There are questions to be answered first and last by you, the actor. The answers do *not* come out of rehearsal as much as they come out of *you*, from your own imagination. Try to answer these questions from the viewpoint of Irina or Tusenbach in the exercise that follows.

EXERCISE 7–1

THE BARON'S FAREWELL I

The following scene is the famous farewell between Baron Nikolai Tusenbach and Irina in Chekhov's *The Three Sisters*. The Baron has long sought Irina's hand in marriage, and she has finally, although reluctantly, consented. Overjoyed, he resigns his army post and prepares for married life as a civilian. But there is a problem; yesterday an impatient and somewhat deranged Army officer challenged the Baron to a duel, and the Baron was forced to accept the challenge. The duel is to take place momentarily, and the Baron fears (correctly, as it turns out) that he will be killed. He does not want Irina to know about the duel, however. In the scene, the characters' deepest thoughts are expressed only indirectly, and the lines of dialog only suggest their inner feelings.

1. Study the scene and prepare the role of Tusenbach or Irina depending on your sex. Both characters are young adults.

2. Underline your lines; in a different color, underline your line cues; in a third color, underline your action cues where they differ from the line cues. Analyze the logic of your speeches, and imagine the thoughts that connect them. Memorize your part, noting the thought linkages, that make memorization come easier. Make notes toward a VOTEsheet for the part.

3. In a subsequent class, pair with a partner and play the scene *without* rehearsal, just as you played the contentless scene exercise (Lesson 3). Then switch partners and play it again.

The scene:

IRINA: *(Referring to the army brigade leaving town)* Our town will be empty now.

TUSENBACH: Dear, I'll come right back.

IRINA: Where are you going?

TUSENBACH: I have to go to town, then . . . to see my comrades off.

IRINA: It's not true . . . Nikolai, why are you so distraught today? *(Pause)* What happened yesterday near the theatre?

TUSENBACH: *(With an impatient gesture)* In an hour I'll be back and will be with you again. *(Kissing her hand)* My beloved . . . *(Looking into her face)* It's five years now I've loved you, and somehow I can't get used to it, and you seem always more beautiful to me. What lovely, wonderful hair! What eyes! I'll take you away tomorrow, we will work, we'll be rich, my dreams will come true. You shall be happy. Only there is one thing, one thing: You don't love me.

IRINA: That's not in my power! I'll be your wife, faithful and obedient, but it's not love, what is there to do? *(Crying)* I have never been in love—not once in my life. Oh, I've dreamed so of love. I've dreamed of it a long time now, day and night, but my soul is like some fine piano that's locked and the key is lost. *(A pause)* You have a restless look.

TUSENBACH: I haven't slept all night. There is nothing in my life so terrible that it could frighten me, and only that lost key tortures my soul—won't let me sleep. Say something to me. *(A pause)* Say something to me . . .

IRINA: What? What shall I say? What?

TUSENBACH: Something.

IRINA: That's enough! That's enough! *(A pause)* *

TUSENBACH: What nothings in life, what foolish trifles will take on meaning suddenly, for no reason at all. You laugh at them as you've always done, you consider them nothings, and yet you go on and

---

*For brevity, the exercise may end at this point if desired.

feel that you haven't the strength to stop. Oh, let's not talk about that! I feel gay. I see these firs, maples, birches now as if I were seeing them for the first time and they are all looking at me curiously and waiting. What beautiful trees and what a beautiful life there should be under them! *(A pause)* I must go. It's time. . . . There's a tree that's dead, but it still waves with the others in the wind. So it seems to me even if I die, I'll still share in life somehow or other. Good-by, my dearest . . . *(Kissing her hands)* The papers you gave me are lying on my table, under the calendar.

IRINA: But I'm going with you.

TUSENBACH: *(Alarmed)* No, no! *(Going quickly, stopping in the alley)* Irina!

IRINA: What?

TUSENBACH: *(Not knowing what to say)* I didn't drink any coffee today. Tell them, so that they'll make me some. *(He goes quickly out.)*

The scene in Exercise 7–1 is famous precisely because the characters don't say exactly what they're thinking, and because the logic of their speeches is highly dependent on their unexpressed thoughts about their needs for each other, and about their reflections on love, nature, life, and death, in the context of their possible future relationship. In memorizing either part, you will be forced to come to grips with these emotions merely through the memorization process. In playing the part without rehearsal, and with different partners, you will see how your character's thinking is affected by the behavior of the other characters—as played by your acting partners.

You will probably want to explore this scene further. Why has Irina accepted the Baron's proposal if she doesn't love him? Or does she love him? Why does the Baron rhapsodize about the trees? The scene itself does not answer these questions; it merely poses them. You must read the entire play, of course, before proceeding further with this exceptionally complex and lovely scene.

Summary

The first step in presenting a scene is to choose, edit, and memorize material. Once a text is chosen and edited, and the actors each have precise and identical copies, memorization can begin. During memorization, you will be studying the part and beginning your VOTEsheet analysis by necessity—as you explore the logic of your character's thinking and the connection of your character's speeches with each other, and with the "action cues" that prompt them. A memorized scene can be presented without rehearsal and with different partners, revealing a good deal about the spontaneous behavior that may be part of the scene's situation and interaction.

Studying and Rehearsing

Studying

Studying is the private part of actor preparation; rehearsal, the public part.

Study leads you to the character: what your character wants, fears, expects, and is capable of trying. Go back to Lesson 6, fill out the VOTEsheet, and determine the main lines of your character's struggle. *This you do entirely by yourself,* subject, of course, to your director's guidance when a director is present. Your acting partner is *not* your consultant in developing your VOTEsheet; your acting partner's concern is his or her own character, his or her own VOTEsheet. The best acting scene will be the result of a dramatic confrontation between individually ambitious (and vulnerable) characters. Their individualism must be nurtured in private: hence the importance of private study in first approaching the role.

Rehearsing

Rehearsals are the opportunity to practice and develop the dramatic confrontation between your character and your acting partner's character.

Rehearsal originally meant "re-harrow," or "cultivate the field again." The French word for rehearsal is *répétition.* Thus rehearsal is a process by which you repeat your parts until they are learned —and until the lumps are broken down.

In a play production, rehearsals are under the control of the director. Ordinarily the early rehearsals involve lectures or discussions on the play's meaning and the production concepts, and the development of the play's staging. In preparation for a classroom acting scene, ordinarily no individual controls the rehearsal; therefore you and your partner must develop a working method together.

Undirected Rehearsals

Your first task in an "undirected" rehearsal is to establish a rehearsal schedule and exchange addresses and telephone numbers for staying in contact between rehearsals. Once scheduled, no rehearsal time should be changed except for reasons of emergency (or *mutual* convenience). If possible, your schedule should include at least one rehearsal in the space where your scene will be presented; if that is impossible, then rehearse at least once in a similar space. Also, at least one rehearsal should involve all the props you will use and the clothes you will wear in the scene. Ordinarily, this will be the last rehearsal.

Usually you will begin your first rehearsal by "running lines" with your partner. This means sitting or standing apart from others, and saying your (memorized or partly memorized) lines to each other as directly as possible.

Don't "try" to act! On the other hand, don't try to maintain a complete monotone. Inevitably, as you run lines, you will begin to "slide" into the scene, to slide into acting. This "sliding" will show you the continuity between yourself and your character and help you to discover yourself, quite naturally, in your role.

As soon as you can comfortably run lines without looking at your script, discard it and, without consideration yet of staging the scene, begin to run lines in a variety of imaginary locales. Run your scene while seated at a lunch counter, or while jogging, or while lolling on a sofa. Do the scene while washing the (real) dishes, or while eating a (real) hamburger, or while changing your (real) outer garments. As you do this, even though the actions may be irrelevant to the content of the scene, the lines will become more natural to you, and you will find yourself, by necessity, studying your partner very freshly each time. As you rehearse in this manner, the relationship between you and your acting partner—as characters in the scene—will grow and deepen of its own accord.

Between rehearsals, you will naturally want to talk about the scene. How much should you discuss or analyze what's happening? The perhaps surprising answer: not much. Analysis may diminish the freshness of the scene and superimpose a director-actor relationship onto your character-character one. Analysis tends to forge a "playing agreement" that may defeat the dramatic confrontation your scene is supposed to portray. Try to find out more about your scene and your characters by rehearsing rather than by analyzing. Do your best thinking about the scene *while it's going on*.

Above all, never try to direct your partner, and never allow your partner to direct you. No matter how experienced you feel you are, or how well you think you understand your partner's role, or how well you know "how the scene should play," your job is to act your role to the fullest, not to play both roles at the same time. As an actor, you will shape the scene from within, not from the outside. When actors try to direct each other, the scene inevitably becomes self-conscious, and the emotions and rhythms become "fixed" rather than free-flowing. An acting scene is not a directed performance, and it should not try to look like a directed performance; its goal is to bring out the most intense, honest, vivid, and dramatic interaction between the two of you. No one will mind, at this stage in your work, if the outward form does not resemble the Royal Shakespeare Company production.

Between rehearsals you should talk about the context of the scene. How old are we (characters)? How long have we known each other? Where did we go to school? Where did we first meet? How rich are our parents? What are we wearing? Where do we work? And so forth.

You can also tell your acting partner which of his or her behaviors stimulate you emotionally. "You really frighten me when you look at me that way," or "I get very charged up when you do that"—with such remarks you can encourage your partner to do the kind of things that "get to you" and will, in turn, make your own performance more exciting.

Remember, you want your acting partner to surprise you. You also want your partner to get under your skin: to annoy you, to interest you, to unnerve you, to frighten you, to attract you, or to disgust you. Intellectual analysis, well-intentioned and brilliant though it might be, will tend to level out the emotions and eliminate the surprises in your scene. Rehearsal, remember, is "harrowing." It should plow up the field, not smooth it down.

At this point, you can also begin to talk of the staging elements of your eventual presentation. Where should the scene be set? What props should be used? What should you wear? These are decisions you must reach together, preferably after some experimenting during rehearsals. Gradually you will add these elements to the rehearsal process.

Between rehearsal periods—and sometimes during short rehearsal breaks—you should go over your VOTEsheet by yourself, adding to and changing or refining your character's goals as the rehearsals seem to suggest. The rehearsal period is an opportunity for experiment, and nothing that comes out of the study should be treated as sacrosanct—particularly if it does not prove stimulating or effective in rehearsal. During rehearsal you will certainly want to try out various tactics: Which ones work best on your acting partner? If he or she proves impassive to your threats, or immune to your charms, don't simply complain: Try *new* threats or *new* charms, and *keep trying* until you find tactics that actually work. Sure, you can "direct" your partner outside the scene, and force him or her to fake the sort of response you want—but how much better it is to find the action that will provoke a *real* response. If you find your partner difficult, all the better; it will simply make you work harder within the scene, which will translate as acting intensity.

Acting, like life, is not easy; and acting that represents life should not be easy. The most common fault of beginning actors is to try to stage-manage a scene by agreement ("I'll raise my fist and you run toward the door," "I'll smile and you throw your arms around me and give me a kiss") rather than really working hard to make their intended character victories come about. In life, the other guy doesn't always agree—not, at least, without some struggle on your part.

Gradually your rehearsal will take on the form of the "finished" scene. Some actors feel comfortable only when every gesture, every inflection, and every pause is rehearsed to repeatable perfection. Others like to keep the scene much more fluid and improvisational—particularly insofar as the movement, timing, and emotional levels are concerned. For a fully produced play, the "repeatability" is a crucial factor, inasmuch as lighting cues, scenery shifts, and special effects must be timed precisely to your actions. In a classroom presentation, on the other hand, it is almost always best to keep the scene fairly fluid, concentrating on the vitality and intensity of the character-to-character interaction rather than the fine points of performance finesse.

How much rehearsal do you need? The theatre has a rule of thumb, which is the one hour per one minute ratio: A standard two-hour play would be professionally rehearsed in three forty-hour weeks, or an hour's rehearsal for each minute of stage time. Thus, a five-minute scene might be considered well-rehearsed in five hours. But a produced play requires attention to many technical details that are rarely encountered in the classroom scene. It is not unreasonable, therefore, to plan a rehearsal schedule of three one-hour periods for a five-minute scene, provided that the actors do their individual study beforehand and are off book at least midway through the *first* rehearsal.

You should be aware that a great deal of professional film and television acting, some of the highest quality, is performed with virtually *no* formal rehearsal. Indeed, in many cases, actors in film/television media are hired for one day only, making any real rehearsal simply impossible. Even in the live theatre, understudies frequently perform publicly without any rehearsal. Rehearsal can be most useful to an actor, but there is no absolute minimum length of rehearsal time that must precede performance. Rather, the rehearsals should be used to build the basis for strongly pursued stage interactions and to create the basic structure of a staged acting scene.

Rehearsal Alternatives

Repetitive rehearsals are not, of course, the only means of preparing for your performance.

Improvisation—where you and your partner enact your parts, improvising lines and movement rather than relying on the memorized text—is a time-honored way of immersing yourself in the scene's situation and developing the intensity of the relationship without regard to the precise plotting or character development of the script. You may choose to improvise the situations that precede your scene or follow it. Improvisation takes its own direction and gives you the opportunity to explore the characters in the fullest possible range. Often, particularly in a scene set in a remote period, improvisation unlocks the deepest meaning of a scene's emotional conflict and makes you aware of the depth of feeling your character experiences.

Massage provides an opportunity to get close to your partner physically and lose your natural inhibitions about touching and being touched—inhibitions that can stand in the way of developing a strong relationship onstage. With your partner lying down, gently "stretching" his or her head, limbs, muscle mass, fingers, and toes is an excellent actor massage that helps to align the spine and promote a more relaxed intimacy that can lead to emotionally vivid acting. Mutual massage can also break down tension and establish trust in its place. Trust is a valuable ingredient in any scene.

Partying, believe it or not, also is a good preparation for acting. Acting is serious business, of course, but it is not necessarily a businesslike-business, and the need to establish personal rapport and sympathy is often critical to a scene's success. Partying cannot replace rehearsals, but getting together "just for the fun of it" can supplement more serious work perfectly. Sensing your partner's joys and excitements helps you share in his or her idealism and expectations; it helps you to know your partner as a whole person and interact with him or her more effectively and with deeper feeling. Actors, of course, are not necessarily any more gregarious than the rest of the population, but long-lasting professional friendships seem to be particularly characteristic of the acting society.

EXERCISE 8–1

THE BARON'S FAREWELL II

Before beginning this exercise, you should have read *The Three Sisters* and memorized the Tusenbach-Irina scene in Exercise 7–1.

Now select a partner and study and rehearse the scene for class presentation. Between rehearsals, revise your VOTEsheet and make notes on how you feel the scene is developing. Experiment with the concept of "shaping the scene from within"—that is, try to get the most out of your acting partner while rehearsing, not by telling her or him how to act the other role. After three to five hour-long rehearsals, and one or more "alternative" rehearsals, present the scene. How was it different from the unrehearsed "first-time" presentation? Was it better in rehearsals than in its class presentation? (The usual answer is yes. But you will learn to overcome self-consciousness as you become accustomed to acting in front of an audience.) More important, were you able to use the rehearsals to improve your understanding—and hence your acting—of your role?

Summary

Rehearsal, the public part of scene preparation, comes from a word implying repetition and digging; rehearsals are opportunities to go over your part several times, exploring and experimenting as you go. Rehearsals should enable you to slide into your role rather than jumping into a fully theatrical performance, and your rehearsals should encourage improvisational exploration of your character-to-character relationship. You should make no attempt to direct your partner in rehearsals, but should try to shape the scene by acting it. There is no rule governing the number of rehearsals that are necessary, but three to five hours for a five-minute scene is a good starting point. Alternative methods of rehearsing include open improvisation and other person-to-person interactions tangent to the actual material.

Self-Staging

Stage Directions

In a produced play, the staging is generally initiated by the director, and the setting is fixed before rehearsals begin.

In a scene for class, *you* will determine where the scene is set, what sort of furniture and props will come into play, where the doors will be, and what the movement will be like. You will also create the behavior of the action: the laughing, drinking, smoking, walking, standing, and sitting that may or may not be particularly specified by the text.

You should know that the published acting editions of most plays contain stage directions added by the original stage manager, which do not carry the authority of the playwright. You need not follow them, and in fact you should feel free to disregard *all* stage directions except those that are explicitly required to further the plot. You are certainly not going to have the Broadway set for your scene, and the original stage directions were chosen for their effectiveness in the context of the original production's scenery, lighting, and overall stylization. In your classroom presentation, the staging should simply liberate and enhance your acting. You should cross out the written stage directions (and stage descriptions), therefore, and start afresh.

Creating the Locale

The tendency among beginners is to have two characters sitting or standing somewhere talking to each other. There may be scenes where this arrangement is the best one possible, but they are rare. In the first place, "somewhere" is just too abstract for the actor's necessary sense of specificity. Where is this somewhere? What kind of place is it? How far away is the door? How many places are there to sit? What sort of objects are there? A scene set in a kitchen can, for example, be played at the sink, at a table, by the refrigerator door, at the silverware drawer, on the floor, against the wall, or in various combinations of these locations. Which one or ones make the scene's interaction more intense? More believable? More confrontational? Look at this "kitchen scene" from Arthur Miller's *Death of a Salesman:*

WILLY: I hope we didn't get stuck on that machine.

LINDA: They got the biggest ads of any of them!

WILLY: I know, it's a fine machine. What else?

LINDA: Well, there's nine-sixty for the washing machine. And for the vacuum cleaner there's three and a half due on the fifteenth. Then the roof, you got twenty-one dollars remaining.

WILLY: It don't leak, does it?

LINDA: No, they did a wonderful job. Then you owe Frank for the carburetor.

WILLY: I'm not going to pay that man! That goddam Chevrolet, they ought to prohibit the manufacture of that car!

LINDA: Well, you owe him three and a half. And odds and ends, comes to around a hundred and twenty dollars by the fifteenth!

WILLY: A hundred and twenty dollars! My God, if business don't pick up I don't know what I'm gonna do!

LINDA: Well, next week you'll do better.

WILLY: Oh, I'll knock 'em dead next week. I'll go to Hartford. I'm very well liked in Hartford. You know, the trouble is, Linda, people don't seem to take to me.

This lovely scene—seemingly innocuous dialog culminating in a shocking revelation and reversal—can take on many different colors depending on where in the kitchen the actors choose to play it. Suppose Willy is fixing himself a cup of coffee, or

Linda is polishing the knives, or Willy drinking a glass of milk, or Linda sitting at the table going over the bills. Suppose there is a drawer to be slammed shut, a drink to be put down a bit too sharply, a knife to be handled a bit too longingly. What happens if Willy is sitting and Linda standing—or the other way around? Suppose Willy kicks the refrigerator (the "machine" he mentions in his first line), hurts his toe, and sits—what response will that stimulate in Linda? If Linda walks out of the room while saying "next week you'll do better," what response will that stimulate in Willy? There are no right or wrong answers to these questions, no right or wrong ways to stage the scene. But there are self-stagings that will encourage stronger acting from both partners.

Movement and Stage Business

Movement is not essential in any scene, and movement inserted in a scene merely to "liven things up" does more harm than good. But natural movement that comes out of the scene's situation, and out of the interplay of the characters, can evoke stronger, fuller, and deeper acting from both partners. Movement, because it involves the whole body—muscles, skeleton, internal organs—makes the actor organically active, and involves the actor bodily in acting a role—and embodying a character.

Moreover, movement creates a general context for the acting of a play's transitions, discoveries, climaxes, and reversals. Learn Willy's last line in the above scene, for example, and give it while jogging. Inevitably, you will stop jogging—or at least change the rhythm of your jogging—as you start to say, "You know, the trouble is, Linda . . ." Jogging would (probably) be inappropriate behavior for Willy in this scene, of course, but drying dishes, playing solitaire, or flipping a coin wouldn't be.

Movement also creates opportunities for physical contact and interaction that would not occur if the actors simply decided to sit down and play the scene "in place." Willy jogging with Linda would have to reach out and stop her if he decided to stop himself. If Willy were playing solitaire, Linda could help him make a move ("Well, next week you'll do better") and Willy could grab her arm ("Oh, I'll knock 'em dead next week") and then let go of it ("You know, the trouble is . . ."). The physical interaction will stimulate emotional interaction, and give contour to the evolving relationship between the characters.

The importance of finding good stage business has long been recognized by directors; it can prove immensely helpful to actors as well. Stage business provides a physical movement that becomes the baseline of a scene—and usually a baseline that is more interesting than two actors facing each other and talking. Well-chosen stage business has several beneficial functions; it relaxes you because it starts you "doing something"; it tones you up because it keeps you busy; it keeps you mentally alert because it doubles your focus; and it intensifies your responses, which are reflected unconsciously in your stage business activity. If Linda is adding up figures in an account book in the *Death of a Salesman* scene, the way she fingers her pencil will reflect her growing anxiety. If Willy is nursing a cup of coffee, his divided interest between drinking his coffee (something good) and paying his bills (something bad) will keep his feelings jumbled, and his reactions will be far more volatile (and interesting) than if he simply listens to Linda in a stupor.

One of the best things about stage business is that it makes stillness, when it occurs, "pay off." When Willy stops jogging, or stops drying dishes, or when Linda puts her pencil down and quietly looks at him, both actors and audience will feel the depth of the moment far more than if both actors were static to begin with. So try to find appropriate and dramatically stimulating business possibilities for your scene: How will your acting develop if you play the scene at the piano? At the bar? At the barber shop? In the men's room? At the basketball court? While walking? While exercising? While playing solitaire? While getting dressed?

Interesting Positions

In the earliest days of Greek sculpture—the era art historians call "archaic" or "preclassical"—statues of humans showed the figure erect, facing forward, one foot about six inches ahead of the other. As sculpture developed, the human form was shown in more and more dynamic positions, until by the late Renaissance it was depicted in all its writhing, twisted possibilities. The same sort of development happens in acting. The beginning actor is usually "stiff" and adopts rigid, symmetrical, square-shouldered positions, often sitting or standing primly, facing his or her partner head-on. You must learn to break down this stiffness. Even positions fixed by the situation (a witness in a witness chair, a family at the dinner table, Prometheus chained to his rock) can be explored with an eye to the possible dynamics of your physical positioning.

In an acting class, you are usually limited to the furniture on hand for the staging of your scenes. A sofa is a wonderful luxury to have on hand for that purpose, for it permits thousands of positions—lying, sitting, sitting on the sofa's arms or back, and innumerable combinations of these. An armchair also offers a great many possibilities. But even without these, you should be able to use furniture, props, and arrangements of your scene locale to create opportunities for positions that are physically interesting and challenging. What happens if your partner's head is in your lap? Or you are sitting on a chair while your partner lies on the floor (beneath you) and then rises to stand (above you)?

During a class break, if you have one, or after an exercise when your classmates have not yet returned to their seats, look at the positions people take when just talking or lolling around. Aren't they interesting? Generally, their positions are very interesting, and much more dynamic (even in repose) than the positions these same people take in their first acting scenes. Our bodies are *naturally* dynamic and interesting, but we naturally stiffen into "sit up straight" positions when we find ourselves on public display. You should learn to transcend this tendency in your own work.

Reaching the Audience

One of the major responsibilities of the stage director is to block (stage) the play in order to make the lines and the plot very clear to the audience. This means taking into account the size of the auditorium, the orientation of the stage to the house, the vocal projection of the actors, the lighting, and a myriad other factors. In an acting class, this responsibility is yours. Certainly the class audience must be able to see and hear your scene adequately if they and the instructor are to give you a valuable critique.

Your job in staging your scene is to make it reach the audience.

Try to ascertain, first of all, what the instructor expects for the physical orientation of the scene. Some instructors like to have scenes performed in the round, others on a proscenium stage or in a proscenium format; still others will permit you to place the audience as you wish. In any event, this factor is your primary consideration. How far away is the audience going to be? In the scene exercise, how important is full projection? If there is a chance that, at this stage of your work, full projection can be achieved only with a loss of honesty and realism, which should you go for? Ask your instructor for guidance.

In a proscenium format—that is, with the audience on one side of you—your staging pattern should keep your face more on the downstage (audience-facing) side than on the upstage side. There are many ways of doing this without being blatant about it. You can enter the scene diagonally from the rear. You can seat yourselves at the upstage sides of a square table placed diagonally to the audience. You can loll about on a sofa placed diagonally toward the audience, with your head on the upstage side and your partner sitting on the upstage part of the sofa back and facing you (and then falling into your lap). You can look out an imaginary window facing into the audience. Your partner can come to you, put his or her arms around you as you both look out, first facing straight ahead and then turning to each other. These are all standard directorial techniques that you can adopt to get your scene out to the audience while at the same time playing very intensely and honestly with each other; they are immensely preferable, from an acting point of view, to standing face to face with your partner while speaking your lines.

EXERCISE 9–1

SETTING THE STAGE

Memorize and rehearse, without staging, either the Tusenbach-Irina scene in Exercise 7–1 or the Willy-Linda scene in this lesson. Disregarding for the time being the author's setting (in *The Three Sisters*, a veranda; in *Death of a Salesman*, a kitchen), set up props and furniture representing one of the following:

1. A piano

2. A ballet *barre*

3. Beachtowels at the beach

4. A writing desk

5. A living room couch

6. An outdoor cafe

Start your staging with one character seated, one standing, and with Willy or Irina actively doing something with regard to the "set" (for example, playing the piano, doing exercises at the *barre,* sunning oneself, writing a letter, lying on the couch reading, drinking a glass of wine or beer or tea). Then stage the scene by exploring all possibilities for business, physical dynamics, and projection. Have a friend watch and make suggestions.

Then return to the author's setting and restage the scene, finding business derived from that setting, and maintaining the opening position of one character seated (or lying) and one standing.

What positions give you the greatest sense of involvement? Of freedom? Of power? Of rapport with your partner? These are the positions you will want to find in your acting scenes. What positions make you feel inhibited? Self-conscious? Tense? Isolated? Stiff? These are positions to avoid.

Summary

Your self-staging should not be an attempt to give a final staging patina to your scene. Rather, it should create a movement pattern that brings out the best acting from you: the most vigorous struggle to achieve your victory, the most provocative tactics, the most enthusiastic pursuit of your character's goals. Staging for your scene should be chosen mainly because it stimulates *you:* It makes you work harder—it requires that you be more forceful, more seductive, more amusing, or more inspirational—to get what your character wants.

Choices

The Need for Choices

The exciting actor differs from the unexciting actor chiefly because of the quality of her or his acting choices—what the actor chooses to play and chooses to do during a scene. These choices are not always apparent in the lines; in fact, sometimes the choice is not even *mentioned* in the lines. For example:

VERSHININ: If they are not giving us any tea, let's at least philosophize.

TUSENBACH: Yes, let's. What about?

VERSHININ: What about? Let's dream . . . for example, of the life that will come after us in two or three hundred years.

TUSENBACH: Well? After us they will fly in balloons, styles of coats will change, they will discover the sixth sense, perhaps, and develop it; but life will remain quite the same, a difficult life, mysterious and happy. And after a thousand years, man will be sighing the same: "Ah, how hard it is to live!" and meanwhile, exactly the same as now, he will be afraid of death and not want to die.

VERSHININ: How shall I put it? It seems to me everything on earth must change little by little and is already changing before our eyes. In two or three hundred, eventually a thousand years— it's not a matter of time—a happy life will come. We won't share in that life, of course, but we are living for it now,

working, well—suffering; we are creating it—and in that alone
lies the purpose of our being and, if you like, our happiness.

(Anton Chekhov, The Three Sisters)

This conversation between two young military officers seems
straightforward enough, but if actors simply played the superficial "philosophizing," they would miss the point of the scene
entirely—which is that both officers are "performing" for the
women they love, who are listening in the background. Tusenbach is trying to persuade Irina (who is playing cards elsewhere
in the room) that his life is terribly hard without her; Vershinin
is suggesting to Masha—without saying it in words—that she
could find happiness with him. This is, then, not a scene of
philosophizing at all, but of romance—even though the romantic characters don't speak to each other.

This understanding should dictate Vershinin's and Tusenbach's tone of voice, deportment, gestures, smiles, enthusiasm,
wittiness, bravura, sensitivity, and stage business. And yet none
of this appears in Chekhov's stage directions! Thus the actors
must choose whether to be sitting, standing, dancing, moving,
laughing, singing, joking, moralizing, parodying, pontificating,
balancing on one foot, smoking a cigar, looking around the
room, or whatever combination of those and other choices will
provide the basic *inner and outer* action of the scene, for which the
spoken lines are merely a convenient vehicle.

Good Choices

Good choices are bold, scary, and exciting. They are choices
you can pursue vigorously and with enthusiasm. They involve
other characters as well as yourself. They are both physical and
psychological: They involve your mind and body and your partner's mind and body. Good choices stimulate your own emotions when you play them with your partner.

Bad choices are safe, sane, and ordinary. They do not tax
your feelings; they provoke in you no joy; they neither frighten
nor absorb you. Purely intellectual choices involve neither your
feelings nor your body. They are easy and pedestrian. They are
self-contained, involving no one but you.

Good choices might be:

I want her to love me.

I want him to cry.

I want him to wet his pants.

She might kill me.

She might kill herself.

I want her to kill herself.

These are not exaggerations. Plays are about moments of crisis, not casual conversations about ordinary day-to-day events. In the theatre, even seemingly casual conversations, such as Vershinin's and Tusenbach's above, will lead into life-changing decisions. (Because of what happens in that scene, Vershinin will have an affair with Masha, and Tusenbach will die before the play is over.)

Bad choices might be:

I want to express myself.

I want her to understand my position.

I want to persuade him to agree with me.

I worry that he won't agree with me.

I am afraid of losing.

I want to win.

I want him to admire me.

These are bad choices not because they are wrong, but because they are not very provocative—to you, the actor, or to the audience. They are general rather than specific, intellectual rather than psycho/physical, and self-contained rather than interactive.

As you can see, sex and violence predominate in the good choices; rational decision-making predominates in the bad choices. Because of the perennial furor over sex and violence in the cinema and on television, it might seem ironic to focus on them as good choices for the actor. But the furor has obscured the obvious: *All* great plays involve sex or violence—or, more likely yet, sex *and* violence. This means not only the great trage-

dies—*Prometheus, Medea, King Lear,* and so forth—but great comedies, farces, and melodramas, or for that matter, bad comedies,
farces, and melodramas. Indeed, the theatre was created to help
humankind come to terms with life's big mysteries: the ecstacy
of sex, the terror of violence—and sometimes the terror of sex,
the ecstacy of violence—and for an actor to avoid these mysteries is to miss not only the opportunity of acting but the whole
point of the theatre.

In making your acting choices, therefore, *always look for a
sexual interest, and always look for a potential terror.* Sexual includes
romance, success, dominance, and even wealth, all of which can
have sexual components. Terror includes embarrassment, confusion, humiliation, and pain, all of which have a terrifying component. Make choices that inspire your feelings, that get under
your (and your acting partner's) skin. Choices that are merely
rational—no matter *how* rational—will not lead to an exciting
performance.

Choose to find your partner interesting. Your partner is an interesting person. Did you know that? Often we don't even notice. We
think "He (she) is 'just' my acting partner." But that acting partner is a caring, feeling, fearing, loving person; sometimes frustrated, sometimes beautiful, sometimes explosive. Your partner
is capable of violence, brilliance, panic, and schizophrenia; your
partner *could* become your lifelong lover or your bitterest enemy
or both.

These statements are facts. It is up to you not to dispute
them, but to work them into your acting relationship. Finding
your partner fascinating, or scary, or adorable, or exhilarating is
a *choice,* and a choice you must learn to make.

You must choose, therefore, to find your partner interesting:
to make him or her a worthy opponent if the scene involves
opposition, or a luring sex object if the scene involves sexual
attraction, or a frightening menace if the scene involves terror.
Only if you give your acting partner the potential for love, for
violence, for brilliance, and for explosive surprise will you truly
get involved with him or her on a personal level.

There are many ways to "discover" how interesting/fascinat-
ing/scary your partner really is. Conversation is the most obvious, particularly personal conversation about growing up, about
one's plans for the future, that sort of thing. It is important to

see your acting partner as an evolving person like yourself, not as a fixed stereotype. Your acting partner has a past and a future, she or he is in flux, is changing, is still an *unfinished* human being. The more you realize this, the easier it will be to play dynamically with your partner, to try to work your magic on him or her, and allow his or her magic to work on you.

Study your partner while you rehearse your scene. How does she or he react to your threats in the scene? To your smiles? To your touch on her or his neck? You don't need to come up with answers to these questions. Indeed, they are fundamentally unanswerable in a real relationship. You need only to search them out and to recognize the mystery, complexity, and fascinating profundity of your acting partner. Even in a seemingly commonplace scene, this awareness will prove beneficial.

Choose goals (victories) that excite you personally, and physically. The audience will never be excited for you if you aren't excited for yourself. Remember, you are not telling or describing a story, you are *embodying* it; and your body must share in the enthusiasm of your pursuit. Imagine winning your victory in the scene: Would winning make you want to jump up and down? No? Then you have made a poor choice.

Choose fears that frighten you personally and physically. Does it upset you to think that your partner might turn his back on you? How much?

Does it upset you to think that she or he might stick pins under your fingernails? How much?

Which imagined event stimulates the most revulsion in you? The most physical nausea? That is the most powerful image to choose. Using each of these images, play the following line to your partner: "I don't want to see you again." Which image made your voice quiver? Which choice most successfully embodies a touch of fear in the line?

Choose to touch your partner. It is equally logical to touch or not to touch your partner; both choices can be defended in a theoretical analysis. But the best acting choice usually is to touch, out of either anger or affection, or, even better, a mixture of both.

Touching your partner is both physical business and personal contact; it usually intensifies the rapport between actors and deepens the concentration of both partners. More important, it

makes *you* feel more involved in the scene. Therefore, in rehearsing a scene, try to find a reason to

Rub your partner's shoulders or back

Stroke or tousle your partner's hair

Playfully poke your partner with your toe

Take your partner's hand

Grab your partner's wrist

Embrace (hug) your partner

Cuddle your partner from behind

Slap your partner

Reach for your partner's neck

All of these touching actions should be noninvasive; you mustn't
construe your acting assignment as a blanket permission to take
sexual liberties with anyone, or to engage in unrehearsed roughhousing. Still, actors must be prepared to be touched, to hug, to
kiss, and to engage in staged physical combat (with appropriate
training) as part of their artistic work. Your instructor will help
you set appropriate boundaries for this touching if you so require.

Touching your partner need not be overtly sexual, and in
most scenes not directly connected with sexual overtures (a
brother-to-brother scene, for example), touching is obviously a
matter of sharing friendship rather than soliciting romance. But
touching is so fundamental to intense human relationships that it
is invariably useful in acting; there are few acting scenes that
cannot be improved simply by directing the actors to touch each
other in some way during the crucial exchange. Touching the
neck, which is both an erogenous zone and a point of extreme
physical vulnerability, can by itself triple the emotional involvement of both actors in a scene representing, for example, a
lover's quarrel. Try it.

Choose to make contact. Beginning actors often tend to look
away, move away, stare at the floor or ceiling, or turn their
backs on their partners at a scene's crucial moments. This behavior comes partly from a mistaken sense of what "looks theatrical"
and partly from shyness and uneasiness. It is partly a holdover

from adolescence, when major confrontations were avoided by running to your room and slamming the door. In acting, you should never "slam the door."

When someone shouts at you face to face, your blood pumps faster, even if you know "it's only a scene in acting class." That moment when your blood surges forth is a great acting moment; you mustn't waste it in a meaningless pause while you turn your back and compose your response. Beginning actors continually overrate the effectiveness of long pauses, even-tempered responses, and deeply furrowed brows.

Similarly, when someone smiles engagingly at you, making you feel suffused by human warmth of a sort mere stage directions cannot create, you are in a particularly wonderful emotional state for acting.

It is precisely at these moments—when you are a bit flustered, a bit moved, not entirely sure of yourself—that you should maintain eye contact with your partner and say your line. These moments are fleeting; they may last a mere split second, but these moments of deep personal contact provide the human vulnerability that makes acting a lively art.

If you retreat from your partner at that moment, by closing your eyes, staring at the ground, or turning your back in heroic defiance (which usually reads as adolescent pique), you have retreated from the most unique and exciting part of acting: your raw feelings and your own particular sensitivity. Please don't "slam the door" on yourself in this way. When someone shouts in your face, shout back, or try to laugh, or cry, or hug the so-and-so, or all of the above! Don't turn your back; to do so is to turn your back on acting itself.

Choose to try to smile. Most people in most person-to-person situations want to be there, want to be liked by the person they are talking with, want to encourage the other person to be friendly. Consequently, most people *smile* much of the time. Lovers breaking up smile—or try to—as do quarreling siblings, labor negotiators, and conspiring executives. To smile while quarreling gives the quarrel a hidden dimension and suggests the possibility that, at the deepest level, both partners seek a reconciliation. This suggestion is both realistic and dramatically effective because it creates sympathy for the characters. Then, when the smile can no longer be maintained—when it struggles against the tears—your scene develops a powerful poignancy. "I want to smile" is one of life's most universal intentions, since it means "I want to be in a situation which pleases me." Everybody wants that, and therefore it should be one of your victory choices.

Choose to hurry your partner. A good pace usually means a rapid pace; when reviewers dislike a play, they usually say that it was "slow" or that it "dragged." But good pace doesn't mean that you have to speak rapidly. What it does mean is that you must be driving for your victory, and that drive means that you not only "want" it but you want it *now*.

"Pacing up a scene" means that you should try to hurry your partner along somewhat, that you should need to win and win quickly. Taking a pause before your speeches—trying to build up feeling before you speak—not only wastes time, but shows that you're "only acting." In real life, people don't try to build up their emotions before they speak. They speak and then find that they have built up emotion!

Thus, in your preparation, choose to find time's winged chariot at your back. Your scene must have a sense of urgency. Sweep your partner off his or her feet; leave your partner speechless with your dazzling argument; but don't plod along with the facts, or indulge in your feelings, or pose nobly and thoughtfully in the glow of your own magnificence.

Choose to be loud. Nothing infuriates the audience like not hearing, and you certainly know that it is unwise to infuriate the audience, even for the best of reasons.

There are reasons to be loud and reasons to be soft. If you are clever enough, you can always find both. Choose reasons to be loud—at least loud to the point that you can be heard clearly from anywhere in the room.

In scenes where you must be quiet so as not to be overheard by the people upstairs, choose to make the ceiling four feet thick.

In scenes where you tell someone that you love him or her, say it in a way that suggests you don't care if the whole world hears—indeed, say it so that the whole world *does* hear.

In scenes when your anger can be expressed either coolly or explosively, choose to express it explosively.

Remember, you can *justify* the opposite choice perfectly well.

But in most cases, that would justify bad acting; you would win the battle and lose the war. In addition to being heard, the "loud" choices stimulate more feeling from your acting partner, which will return more stimulation to you. The cool, quiet, logical choice, eminently justifiable, leads to uninteresting theatre most of the time, yet it is a seductively "safe" way to play a scene, particularly for the beginning actor. Try the bolder, louder, explosive choices first. They are harder to get out, but more liberating. Later, perhaps with a friend acting as a director to guide you, they may be pruned back. Bold choices taken in rehearsal can prove wonderfully enlightening even if toned down by the time of performance.

EXERCISE 10–1

BOLD CHOICES

Study your VOTEsheet for either the Tusenbach-Irina scene, the Willy-Linda scene, or any other scene you have prepared. Do your listed victories really stimulate you psychologically and physically? Do your fears make you cringe? Are your tactics boldly chosen? Are your expectations vivid and exciting? Did you, in playing those scenes, work to find your partner fascinating? Did you touch your partner? Was the quest for victory an urgent one? Were you able to smile? Were you able to shout?

Go back to one of those scenes and rewrite your VOTEsheet with bolder choices. Then play the scene with your partner, implementing those choices. Find points in the scene—mere moments—when you can be explosive or desperate, or where you can reach out and touch someone. Making bold choices is something that you will learn to do a small step at a time, but those steps can be very important in your development as an actor.

After playing the scene, ask your partner if he or she was more stimulated, more frightened, more attracted, more emotionally *involved* with you than before? Chances are the answer will be yes. And if your partner was more involved, chances are you were also.

Summary

The quality of your acting is determined by the choices you make, what you choose to play. Good choices, which are bold and interpersonal, stimulate the emotions of both you and your partner. Bad choices may be logical, but they are unstimulating emotionally and psychologically. Good choices usually involve implied sex and violence, which invoke mankind's most urgent lusts and terrors. Choose to find your partner fascinating. Choose victories and terrors that affect you personally. Choose to touch your partner, to quicken the pace of your scene, to confront your partner face to face, and to find reasons to be loud rather than quiet or "cool."

Performing

Stage Fright

The time comes when the study is complete, the rehearsals are over, the choices are made: Now you perform your scene publicly.

For most actors, tension, nervousness, and stage fright threaten to cancel out the careful preparation. Even veteran actors experience stress in performance, sometimes extreme stress. Fear of the audience, fear of criticism, fear of rejection, fear of forgetting your lines, and fear of looking foolish are the inhibiting factors that may not even surface until the moment of performance, when their appearance can become immediately debilitating.

How can you avoid this fear? First of all, you should recognize that a certain amount of tension is inevitable and may even be desirable. Many actors reach the fullest level of performance only with the added "danger" of a public audience. Even without consciously holding back in rehearsal, many actors find that the presence of a live audience stimulates them to "let go." The audience can spur an actor's power and belief, much as the cheering crowd can intensify an athlete's performance or a speechmaker's eloquence. There is nothing wrong with making use of the added edge of excitement that an audience provides.

But stage fright—the numbing fear of evaluation by others—can just as easily dampen your enthusiasm, inhibit your movement, constrict your voice, and paralyze your reflexes. Scenes

rehearsed with great passion and fervor can dry up in performance and become mere shadows of their former selves. It is
useless to complain "it was better in rehearsal." Your job is to
learn how to make it better in performance.

Classroom Performance

A good classroom performance requires preparation. First, take
the time to set your scene properly; put the furniture in the
proper place, decide where the (imaginary) door is, where the
stove is, and what real properties are represented by substitute
items. Insofar as necessary, the audience also should be informed
of these requirements of the scene. Then your scene should be
announced, quite briefly, with any essential details not obvious
from the scene itself explained as may be necessary.

Then you and your partner should go to your opening positions and *prepare*.

The duration of that preparation varies according to your instructor's guidelines. Some actors like to take a very long time—
a minute or more. It is to your advantage, however, to learn to
make your preparation in as brief a period as possible—for example five to ten seconds. Though brief, your preparation should
be comprehensive. It should include:

A moment of sheer physical release, perhaps by shaking out
your arms, kicking your legs, doing a full body bend, or
pounding your fist into your hand.

A quick study of your partner, bringing up what you find
most fascinating/scary about him or her.

A flash on what *excites* you in the situation of the scene.
What's the *best* that can happen to your character?

A flash on what *terrifies* you in the situation of the scene.
What's the *worst* that can happen to your character?

A final VOTEcheck, perhaps in this order: "I'm gonna (EX-
PECTATION!) get this (VICTORY!) by doing this and this
(TACTICS) to him/her (OTHER). And I'm gonna get it now!"

Running through this little litany will hurtle you out of your
own person (as an acting student) and into the persona of the

scene. During this quick run-through, you will enter the play, realize the excitement the situation holds for you, see the potential for joy and pain your character faces, and see your acting partner not as a fellow student but as a character for or with whom you have a deep need or quest.

Concentration on the other character, and what you (your character) want that other character to do or to believe, is the best "cure" for stage fright. That concentration focuses your energy, liberates your resources, organizes your choices. It will help you to "forget" the audience, and to shape the scene from within, not from without. It will help to eliminate your "director's eye" that continually stands outside your role, an eye that can only confuse you and dissipate your character's energy.

Things to ask yourself during the performance are not "How am I doing?" or "What is my next line?" but:

Is my partner's face flushed?

Is my partner (my partner's character) telling the truth?

Does he (she) love me?

Will he (she) succumb?

Must I press harder? Softer? Do I have him (her) on the run?

Can I make him (her) listen better? Understand better? Understand *me* better? Care more? Like me better?

The more you concentrate on your partner's character, the less you will be aware of the audience. The more you ask yourself real questions about your partner's character, the more you will be involved in the scene, and the more you will create a real situation.

EXERCISE 11–1

PLAY FOR RESULTS

Go for real results in a scene of your own choosing. If your victory is to make the other character love you, try during the scene to make the other actor love you. If you are trying to scare the other character, scare the actor. Try to create real, *physical* results. Try to make the other actor sweat, relax, smile, laugh, cry, or vomit. Try to make his or her heart palpitate, his or her knees weaken, either in fear or in adoration. Look for results from the other actor, not from the audience. If you generate a response from your acting partner, you will also create an impact on the audience watching you.

Actors legitimately differ on how much on-the-spot spontaneity should enter into actual performance. Certainly any physical action that is potentially violent—such as slapping or pushing—should be well rehearsed and performed *exactly* as rehearsed. Sexual advances should be similarly prepared so that both partners agree on what will and won't be done—and that agreement must be honored in the performance. And certainly, actions in a directed play should be performed as rehearsed, subject to the director's instructions (which may or may not allow for on-the-spot improvisation). But an acting class offers considerable leeway for in-performance improvisation. Frequently actions taken on impulse will be preferable to those carefully rehearsed. Acting class should be a place for experimentation, and you should give yourself ample room for experimenting in the performance mode itself.

You should end your scene by saying "scene" or "curtain" when you finish—allowing a momentary pause after the last line or stage action—and then returning to your seat unless instructed otherwise. This is not the time for grimacing, scowling at your partner, or shrugging as if to say "I guess that wasn't very good, was it?" Learn to respect your work and the work of your partner. Do not offer lame excuses or blame your partner or skulk into the background. If something went horribly wrong in performance, you should certainly be able to ask if you may repeat the scene. If you are asked if anything went wrong, you should tell the truth without accusing anyone: It is appropriate to say "we skipped a section of the text" but unwise to say "Joe dropped his lines." Publicly accusing your partner of ruining the scene will make it more difficult to rework the scene effectively and sensitively.

After performing your scene, you should do a quick review in your mind: Were you concentrating? Were you seeking a victory? Did you move your partner? Were you as concentrated, as intense, as free, and as relaxed as you were in your best rehearsal? If not, why not?

Most important, be prepared to learn from your performance.

Acting class is a place to learn, not to show off your wares. You have worked hard on your part, memorized your text, developed and studied your VOTEsheet, rehearsed your scene, performed with eloquence and vigor, and still you are going to receive criticism. Your classmates may be grudging in their approval. Your instructor may talk darkly about your "problems." Your acting partner may stonewall you from across the room. Where did you go wrong?

You didn't. In acting class, you are learning, but you still have a long way to go.

Summary

Stage fright can affect all actors, and can destroy the result you thought you had achieved in studying, staging, and rehearsing your scene. Proper preparation and intense concentration will help to lessen the effects of stage fright; so will going for physical results in your stage interactions, and keeping your scene improvisational in nonessential matters of blocking and inflection. After a scene, you should leave the stage without apology, and should review your work in terms of your preparation and choices.

Evaluation and Improvement

Helpful Criticism

It is often said of writing that the best writing is rewriting. So it is of acting A scene is not "finished" the first time you act it in front of others. A professionally produced play does not reach its finest form until weeks or months into its run; it takes a long time for acting to ripen and mature. As an actor, you will need a chance to prune your excesses, probe your strengths, and polish your rough edges.

Most scenes will improve markedly following judicious critique and reworking if you respond to the criticism positively and engage yourself in the acting process more fully than before.

The first thing to realize after a critique of your scene—particularly after a harsh critique—is that you weren't really *terrible*. Most of us overreact to negative remarks; rare indeed is the actor who has not quit the profession a hundred times (momentarily, at least) after a waspish review or a sneering criticism, or even after the damnation of faint praise.

The second thing to realize, however, is that you probably weren't *wonderful* either. Sure, it would have been better with lights and costumes, or with the right props, or if what's-his-name hadn't forgotten his line and blown your first cue; still, there is work to be done—*your* work—and by doing it you can take giant steps.

The first step is merely listening carefully to the critique, regardless of its source. Certainly there are going to be friends or teachers whose opinions you particularly trust, but the fact is that audiences consist of more strangers than friends, and more nonactors than actors or acting teachers. If *anybody* thinks your scene can be improved, then it probably can be, even if that anybody hasn't a notion as to how to go about improving it. Accept the validity of criticism, even if you don't accept the suggested diagnosis or cure.

As you listen to the criticism, try to answer these questions: What didn't they like? Did they understand the story? The relationship? Could they hear? Most important, did they *care*? That, of course, is the *sine qua non* of theatre: Remember, nobody pays an audience to care about the characters. Making them care is your job. If they didn't care, you haven't succeeded, no matter how "correct" you were.

Many things get said in a critique, some wise, some foolish, but you can learn from them all. Here are some of the most common criticisms with suggestions for your future improvement.

Indicating and indulging are among the most common problems of beginning actors. Although they are not identical problems, both involve the playing of emotions, rather than actions.

Indicating means that you are trying to show the emotions of the character, rather than playing the intentions of the character, or the VOTE of the scene. For example, if in reading the scene you decide the character should be sad and then you play "being sad," you are simply indicating a feeling to the audience, not experiencing it yourself. If, on the other hand, you play "I want him to marry me" and the other character says, "Leave me alone," you will *be* sad, and you don't have to indicate it. Moreover, you might find yourself smiling at that moment (that is, smiling to make him change his mind) rather than "looking sad." Indicating, therefore, is wrong for two separate reasons: because it creates only a simulated emotion which the audience sees through, and because it leads you to make unrealistic and often undramatic choices.

Indulging means playing an emotion for all it's worth, mainly to show off your ability to emote. In the example above, the indicating actor would try to look sad; the indulging actor would whoop out great sobs of anguish and despair. Indulging may make you feel good—or at least feel like you're acting up a

storm—but it is rarely if ever effective, inasmuch as it calls attention to your acting rather than to the character's plight and feelings.

In the theatre, emotion must always be seen to come out of a
character's working through a situation and working through his
or her relationships. The best way to generate emotion is to play
your VOTEsheet boldly and sensitively—that is, to stimulate
your feelings by going directly for real victories, with and
through real people (your scene partners), by using real tactics.
The worst way to generate emotion is to decide which emotion
to portray and then try to manufacture it on your own.

To rework a scene critiqued as indicated or indulged, restudy
the VOTEsheet with an eye particularly to the intention (victory) and interaction with the other actor. For a scene labeled
indulgent, you should also rethink the expectation and figure out
how you can play the scene more positively. In a scene criticized
for indulgence, also consider the time factor. Are you hurrying
your partner adequately? Do you want what you want *now*—
instead of after having a good cry about it? Remember, the
business of the scene is getting what your character wants, not
shedding lots of unnecessary tears in the process.

The scene was boring! Chances are no one will ever say directly
that your scene was boring, but, if the audience was inattentive
and the response unduly faint, you can certainly tell that you
have failed to stimulate the imagination.

Scenes are boring for a variety of reasons—usually because
the choices are timid and impersonal and the underlying relationship is too intellectual, too rational, too expository, too po-
lite. No one gets bored at a sexy scene or a violent one, no
matter how clumsily played. Rethink your choices, and re-exam-
ine the scene for underlying sexual or threatening potential. Get
personal with your partner. Strengthen your tactics. Choose to
make the scene mean something very vivid to you—something
you can get your body into as well as your mind. Intensify your
images of victory and your fantasies of defeat.

I couldn't hear! This common criticism should be met in two
ways. First, restage your scene so that you open out more to the
audience. If it's an intimate scene, put more space between you
and your partner, so that you aren't tempted to whisper. Then
find *reasons* to pick up the scene's volume. If your line is "I love

you" and your inclination is to whisper it, change your inclination: Say the line so that the whole world hears!

Every actor has the obligation to make himself or herself heard at all times. Later in this book, in the "technique" section, there are some specific suggestions that will help you. But at any point in your learning process, you must know that being heard is *your* responsibility—sometimes your first responsibility—as an actor.

When an actor is inaudible to the audience, he or she is often inaudible to the other actors on stage. In other words, the actor is speaking more quietly than he or she would be in the same situation in life (when we are almost never inaudible to the people we're talking to). Stage fright, in any of its many varieties, is the culprit here. Don't ever excuse inaudibility because you were simply "being real." Chances are you were not only being nontheatrical, but you were being unreal as well.

That was great! The most devastating criticism of your scene, sometimes, is unmitigated praise. How do you rework a scene that's been praised to the skies? You must take the praise as a challenge to do even better—and to show yourself that you can do even better.

You must remember that in acting "really great" is not enough, that *no* amount of praise should stop you from working to get deeper and deeper into the actor's art. The actors who are *really* "really great" are one in a million, perhaps one in a generation. Acting is one of those rare professions that truly achieve the rank of art—which means that those practitioners at the very summit of their craft are true immortals, who will be remembered centuries beyond their times. Are you there yet? Of course not. Don't ever let praise, no matter how well-intended or sincere, stand in the way of reaching your highest potential.

Reworking

When you have brought together the criticisms that can help shape your work, and have evaluated your preliminary presentation with your partner, your scene can be rehearsed with an eye to working on the specific problems you were able to isolate. You should experience a sense of freedom at this point; you have already done your scene once; your "first-night" jitters are over, and you can now get on with the work of working on *yourself.* This stage separates the serious student from the casual one, because this is where the hard work begins—work that is not always immediately gratifying, work that does not have the immediate "thrill" of first-time performance.

Choose a fellow student whom you and your partner trust, and ask him or her to observe the reworking rehearsals and judge if the problems seem to be improving. Sometimes the use of a tape recorder or a videotape recorder (if you are fortunate enough to have such equipment) can be most helpful in spotting what the critics saw and correcting it.

Your work will not always improve; occasionally, in fact, it may go downhill. Sometimes the scene just isn't right for you, or you're not ready for it, or the chemistry between you and your partner doesn't work. Don't fall back on excuses, however, and don't be quick to blame. It is your challenge to make every scene yours, every partner your best one, and every role your favorite. No one is going to do this for you, either now or in the future. Reworking should be approached with enthusiasm and dedication, which will not always be rewarded by quickly won success, but must be relentless nonetheless.

Often you will have a chance to re-present a reworked scene. If you have a choice in the matter, you should do so only when you have made a serious effort to rethink your work and have made serious changes in your performance. Don't simply hope for a better mood or a sudden inspiration. Reworking is *working,* and without understanding that, you will have little improvement to show.

EXERCISE 12–1

SCENE PRESENTATION

Select a partner and a scene. Following all the lessons in Part Two, memorize, study, rehearse, stage, and present the scene. Then, guided by a class critique, restudy, restage, re-rehearse, and re-present the same scene in a subsequent class meeting.

Summary

The education of an actor does not end with the first performance; performances are just steps in the learning process. Even good acting can be critiqued, restudied, re-rehearsed, and re-presented to advantage. It is up to you to learn how to take criticism (indeed, how to solicit criticism), how to learn from it, and how to grow by it. Growth is not always continuous and not always easy; the best results involve hard work and little glamor, but the finest acting is always accomplished through relentless diligence.

PART THREE

THE ACTOR'S INSTRUMENT

Parts One and Two are concerned with processes of acting: approaching and preparing dramatic roles. Anyone who has mastered those twelve lessons might be said to have learned "how to act." But becoming an actor means a lot more than learning how to act; it also means becoming a trained and capable acting *instrument*.

The instrument consists of the actor's personal attributes and abilities: appearance, speech and movement capabilities, emotional depths, intelligence, mind-body coordination, sense of timing, sense of drama, and presentational skills. For the actor is both a player and the instrument played; the actor, in other words, plays upon herself or himself in much the same way that a violinist plays upon a violin. Carrying that metaphor one step further, we can say that an actor, like the violinist, can be no better than the instrument—no matter how brilliant his or her approach or dedication to fulfilling tasks. Thus the actor will be rewarded by having a versatile and splendid instrument, or held back by possessing an instrument that is unresponsive, undisciplined, or unable to execute commands with passion, subtlety, excitement, or vivacity.

A fundamental goal for every would-be actor is to develop an instrument that is serviceable for a wide variety of roles. To a certain degree, the actor begins with what is sometimes called "raw talent," although this term is not used as frequently as it was twenty years ago. More often today, the theatre looks for actors who have completed substantial training in actor-training programs. Don't underestimate the amount of training most young American stage actors have as they enter the profession. Typically, a beginning actor at an American regional professional theatre might be expected to have an undergraduate drama degree, a graduate (M.F.A.) or Professional Actor Training Program degree, and two or three years of nonprofessional apprentice work or experience with a semi-professional theatre company. And this is *intensive* training, not casual classes at odd times. Most professional actor-training programs involve students in thirty to seventy hours a week of classes and rehearsals for about three years.

You will not have a professional actor's instrument, then, in a matter of a few weeks or months; nor will Part Three provide you with more than an outline of what you will be working on if you want to pursue acting beyond the beginning level. But the time to start developing your instrument is now. For as you learn how to "play" your instrument, you will want to own a better one.

The Actor's Voice

Breathing

Most people think of the voice as the most important element of the actor's instrument. Asked to name the three most important aspects of acting, Tommaso Salvini, the great nineteenth-century star (and favorite of Stanislavski), said "Voice, voice, and more voice." We have left the oratorical style of Salvini's era, to be sure, but a supple, commanding, and engaging voice is as important as ever.

Voice is not taught in a day; most successful vocal training programs last at least two years, usually three. That's three years of weekly or biweekly classes, and *daily* drills, lasting about an hour each. For we have all been using our voices for years, and much that must be learned requires "unlearning" deep-rooted habits. Moreover, we tend to *resist* that unlearning—deep down, we *like* the way we speak—and one of the actor's hardest tasks is simply learning to believe in the steps necessary to vocal improvement, beginning with learning to breathe.

Breathing is the basis of voice, as it is the basis for life. To *inspire* means to breathe in—as well as to nourish the *spirit* (from the Latin *spiritus*, meaning breath). Breathing is as natural as sleeping—except that you cannot do either unselfconsciously when being stared at by an audience. The actor's goal is simply to breathe naturally while under the pressure of performance—and to provide sufficient lung power to support a voice that may be challenged in acting more than in any other activity, except perhaps in singing.

The *yawn* is the ideal breath because it comes from a relaxed body and because it takes in a substantial quantity of air in an unforced manner. But the actor cannot yawn continuously during a play—except perhaps in Chekhov. When you yawn, chances are, you breathe not from your chest but from your abdomen. And that's where the actor's support breathing must originate. The shallow chest breaths that characterize many beginning actors are the result of tension and self-consciousness— the same sort of tension that would cause shallow breathing if we were to come upon a mugger in a dark alley. Deep body breathing, as deep as possible, gives the voice its fullest support and the body its fullest relaxation.

EXERCISE 13–1

BREATHING FROM THE ABDOMEN

Breathe deeply from the abdomen. Yawn, stretch your arms, and breathe again. Lie down, knees raised, feet and back on the floor. As you breathe, mark the movement of your abdomen, and try to minimize the movement of your chest. Now stand and walk about the room, swinging your arms freely and tasting the air as you breathe it in.

Making Sounds

Oddly, nobody knows for certain how sound is made by the human voice. We do know that the sound is caused by air passing through vibrating vocal folds (also called vocal cords), but whether the air vibrates the folds, like a clarinet reed, or whether the folds, like a violin string, vibrate the air, is a subject of great debate among laryngologists (vocal specialists). However it happens, making sounds is a spontaneously learned phenomenon that the actor must cultivate beyond its everyday function.

The easiest sound to make is the vowel *ah*, and the best way to make it is with the most open-throated and relaxed voice possible. *Ah* is the vowel on which singers and actors routinely warm up their voices, practice scales, and learn to develop resonation and vocal power.

EXERCISE 13–2

SOUNDING

Breathing from the abdomen, say *ah* with each exhalation in any of the following ways:

1. ah hah hah hah hah hah hah
2. pah pah pah pah pah pah pah
3. ahhhhhhhhhhhhhhhhh (sliding down the scale)

   Now, turning the body from side to side, walk around the room and make the same series of sounds, gradually increasing the volume toward the end of each breath:

4. ah hah hah Hah Hah HAH HAH HAHH HAHH! HAHHH!
5. pah pah Pah Pah PAH PAH PAHH PAHH! PAHHH!!
6. ahhhhhhhhhhhHHHHHHHHHHHHHHHHH! (sliding down the scale)

What happens when you increase your volume? Do the vocal folds vibrate faster? No, for faster vibrations would simply increase the *pitch* of your voice (make the sounds go higher on the scale). Volume is a function of how far the vocal folds vibrate, not how fast, which in turn is a function of the air supply under the sound. But a more important determinant of volume in your voice is *resonance.*

Resonance

Resonance is the re-sounding of vocal fold sounds. Re-sounding is a simple phenomenon. Vibration, as of a tuning fork, creates sound, but it also creates other (sympathetic) vibrations, which themselves create sound. Often these secondary sounds, caused by sympathetic vibrations, are louder and fuller than the original tuning-fork sound itself. A tuning fork struck and placed against an empty cigar box, for example, can create an amplified sound far greater than the original because of the resonation of the air within the cigar box.

In the human voice, most of the actual sound is provided by the resonation of three "cigar boxes" inside the vocal apparatus: These are the pharyngeal (throat), oral (mouth), and nasal (nose) cavities that lie above the vocal folds. Air that is first vibrated by the vocal folds then passes through these three empty cavities and creates sympathetic vibrations in both the tissues and the air within them; what emerges is the rich, "full voiced" sound that is characteristic of the peculiar shapes and sizes of each individual's reasonating capacities. Much of our resonation is biologically determined; indeed, "voiceprints" identify individuals as clearly as fingerprints do. But we also have a certain degree of control over the amount of resonation we can produce. If properly exercised, this control can favorably alter the power, timbre, tone, and character of our voices.

Virtually *all* acting students need to improve resonance, simply because the resonance required of the actor is far greater than that required of most other professionals. The actor must be prepared to be full voiced continuously, for several hours at a stretch on a daily basis, *and* must project with authority, *and* must be able to "play upon" an instrument with many subtle gradations of resonance—which itself demands a "resonance reserve" that can be called upon at an instant. Resonation is one way an actor can increase his or her volume and vocal power without straining the voice. Resonation is a way of making your cavities work for you rather than against you—and is therefore a vocal asset that must be carefully cultivated.

But how do you improve your resonance? Relaxation is the first principle; a relaxed throat is an open throat (notice that when we are tense we say we have "a lump in our throat"), and an open throat provides deep, mellow resonance. Thus rolling the head in circles—first one way, then another—is a standard actor's exercise for relaxing the neck and opening up the pharyngeal cavity.

Posture is the second principle: Find the posture that allows your larynx to drop down in the throat, lengthening the column of air (and thereby the pharyngeal resonator) above it. You can feel where your larynx is because it is represented by its forward knob, the "Adam's apple" under your chin. By changing the position of your shoulders, neck, head, and pelvis you can greatly alter the capacity of your throat to open and provide deep resonation.

Contrary to popular belief, there is no "ideal posture" for an actor; every voice has different characteristics, and every body has different internal configurations. In general, all actors will have greater resonation lying on their backs than standing, and with the head thrust forward than with the head held back. But you should try humming and making sounds in a variety of postures to observe how your body and your voice best relate.

Speaking itself is the third principle; an open-jawed, open-mouthed articulation provides greater resonance than a close-lipped, tight-jawed, constricted speech. The vowel *ah* is the standard warm-up vowel for actors and singers because it is made with the jaw fully dropped, providing the greatest oral resonance, and thereby the least demand on the vocal folds themselves. *Ee* and the French *uu* are, by contrast, the least resonant vowels because they require a tightening of the jaw, in the first instance, and a closing of the lips in the second—both practices necessarily reducing the amplitude of resonation.

The *placement* of vowels—that is, the place in the mouth where they are actually formed—determines to some extent how they are resonated. *Ah*, for example, can be fully resonated in the pharynx—or, by widening the lips, tilting the head backward, and raising the larynx, can be shunted more into the nasal cavity, where it will prove more penetrating but also more strident. Nasal resonance creates a harsher sound than pharyngeal resonance, but there are many occasions when a harsh sound is desirable, for reasons of either characterization or projection. The actor should learn how to vary resonance by shifts in the placement of vowels.

EXERCISE 13–3

EXPLORING RESONANCE

1. Stand with your feet slightly spread and your arms held loosely at your sides. Say "pah pah pah pah pah" while twisting your arms and torso lightly side to side. Say it again while tilting your head slowly forward, then back. Say it again while dropping your Adam's apple and forming the sound as deep in your throat as you

can. Say it again while shunting the air out through your nose. Where do you seem to feel the greatest resonance? The mellowest resonance? The most penetrating?

2. Place one hand on the top of your head and say "pee pah pee pah pee." On which syllable do you feel the most vibration? You should feel it on *pee,* which is formed high in the front the mouth and thus generates more head and bone (skull) resonance.

3. Place one hand on the bridge of your nose and say "pah pin pah pin pah pin." Which syllable causes the most vibration? *Pin* will, of course, because it has a nasal vowel and thus creates more nasal resonance than *pah.*

4. Put your hands on your cheeks and say "oo ee oo ee oo" or "oo ah oo ah oo ah." Which vowel creates the most cheek vibration? *Oo* will, because *oo* is formed high in the back of the mouth, making the cheeks a strong resonator for *oo.*

5. Pair with a partner and place your hands on his or her head, nose bridge, and cheeks, by turns, testing his or her resonance as your partner tests yours.

Exercise 13–3 merely shows you what parts of your body are resonating most strongly on particular vowels. Using different vowels, you can also feel resonating vibrations on the collarbone, shoulder blades, forehead, and other parts of the upper body.

A Stageworthy Voice

Speaking is a natural ability, but the actor's voice is cultivated because it must meet certain demands rarely present in everyday life. Stage speaking is to daily conversation what Olympic high hurdling is to the morning jog; it demands training and conditioning as well as above-average gifts. The training is normally carried out under the eye of an accomplished vocal coach, but the conditioning is up to the actor. An hour a day of vocal workout is to the actor what the daily playing of scales is to the concert pianist and daily calisthenics are to the professional athlete. During that conditioning practice, however, the actor can certainly explore his or her own vocal capacities. Sometimes a tape recorder is helpful in developing stageworthy sound. Exercise 13–4 will prove a good starting point for a daily warm-up and exploration.

EXERCISE 13–4
SPEAKING WITH RESONANCE

Warm up by repeating Exercises 13–1, 13–2, and 13–3. Then, by memorizing the phrases below, one at a time, recite each phrase twenty times while exploring your own speaking mechanism by taking different postures, deepening your breathing, and developing new areas of resonance. Do this exercise with a tape recorder or ask a friend to check your results.

Recite these phrases in the shower, if you like. The bathroom will enlarge your resonance, as if you were speaking inside a violin box, and the steam from the shower will keep your vocal folds moist and fresh.

1. "Roll on, thou deep and dark blue ocean, roll!"

2. "Is this a dagger which I see before me,
   The handle toward my hand? Come, let me clutch thee."

3. "Was this the face that launch'd a thousand ships,
   And burnt the topless towers of Ilium?"

4. "Four score and seven years ago our fathers brought forth on this continent a new nation, conceived in liberty, and dedicated to the proposition that all men are created equal."

5. "Oh Romeo, Romeo! Wherefore art thou Romeo?
   Deny thy father and refuse thy name;
   Or, if thou wilt not, be but sworn my love
   And I'll no longer be a Capulet."

6. "Is anybody home?"

7. "Pickle him in pickle sauce!"

8. "You think I'll weep;
   No, I'll not weep.
   I have full cause of weeping; but this heart
   Shall break into a hundred thousand flaws
   Or ere I'll weep. O fool, I shall go mad!"

9. "In the beginning God created the heaven and the earth."

10. "Blasts and fogs upon thee!"

Summary

The actor's voice is primary to his or her acting instrument, and must be trained and conditioned to meet the demands of the theatre. Breathing, the making of sounds, and resonation, the primary tools of the voice, can be cultivated through instruction and exercise.

Stage Speech

Good Diction

Voice produces sound; speech produces language.

The process by which raw vocal sound is transformed into speech begins with *articulation:* the shaping of vocal noise into independent and recognizable units of spoken language, or *phonemes.* There are about forty phonemes in spoken English, plus various phonemic combinations, and the fine actor can speak all of them clearly and distinctly.

Good *diction* has long been considered essential to acting, primarily so that the actor can be clearly heard and understood in all parts of the theatre, and so that the actor can make the most of the author's words and the character's verbal tactics, wit, and persuasive authority. Good diction also means adhering to a standard way of pronouncing words—so that the actors will seem to be "all in the same play," and so that a sense of shared ensemble will be created through the play's words.

In some cultures the standard stage pronunciation requires a lofty tone not ordinarily heard in daily life. The British theatre, for example, favors a "received pronunciation" (you can hear it on the BBC), which has been "received" from the elocutionary arts rather than from normal social conversation. The German theatre, similarly, uses what is called *hochdeutsch* (high German) for most classical and modern plays. The standard American stage speech, however, is simply a refinement of middle American pronunciation, emphasizing naturalness rather than elevated elocution. Learning standard American, as it is called, requires overcoming speech impediments, such as lisping, and eliminating unwanted regional dialects. Learning standard American, then, requires learning the standard speech sounds of the American English language: how to make them and how to use them.

Speech Sounds

Formal speech training begins with identifying the forty basic speech sounds and practicing them in various combinations until complete mastery is achieved. This process takes years. It cannot simply be covered as a single part of a beginning acting class; but an elemental understanding of the basic speech sounds can be achieved quickly, and improvement in speech clarity, power, and precision can be developed after short periods of practice.

The *vowel* sounds of English are divided among those that are formed in the front of the mouth, in the back, and in the middle.

Front Vowels

ee as in beet, heat, feel, see, seize

ih as in hit, tin, rift, pill, skit

ay as in bake, cane, staple, cradle, straight

eh as in bet, sled, when, threat, kept

aa as in cad, bat, stab, pal, add

Back Vowels

ah as in father, Charles, hard, party

a as in wants, pot, God, pollen, bottom

aw as in all, bought, cough, walk, trawler

o as in old, coat, stoke, protest, folk

ŏŏ as in foot, look, tootsie, put, good

oo as in boot, cool, rude, too, food, true

Mid Vowels

uh (stressed) as in cup, rubble, ton, up, none

uh (unstressed) as in above, sofa, pencil, amount, mother

ur as in further, cur, stir, purple, murder

Diphthongs are glides between vowels—two vowels that are sounded in sequence and seem at first hearing to be one.

Diphthongs

ay-ee as in hay, say, feign, weigh, play

eye (ah-ee) as in I, fly, high, sky, mai tai

oy (aw-ee) as in boy, coy, royal, poi, alloy

you (ee-oo) as in ewe, few, putrid, puerile, cue

ow (ah-oo) as in how, now, brown, cow

oh (o-oo) as in slow, throw, go, crow, toe

Learning to speak vowels clearly and cleanly, and to hear the difference between vowels in similar-sounding words (such as *offal* and *awful*), is particularly important to the actor, because the vowel sounds of stage speech carry the tone of the dialog and convey the nuances of a character's tactical pursuits. Also, the vowel sounds of a person's speech often characterize his or her regional background: A trained ear has no trouble identifying the Virginian, the Wisconsinite, the Texan, and the New Englander simply by hearing their *ahs* and *ows*. Actors practice vowel drills in order to develop clarity and strength in their vowels and also to approximate the norm of standard American rather than their native local dialect.

EXERCISE 14–1

VOWELS

Singly or in a group, practice the vowel sounds by reciting the words listed after each vowel on pages 110–111. Notice where the vowel is formed in the mouth. Then speak the diphthongs slowly and see if you can identify which two vowels each diphthong consists of.

EXERCISE 14–2

REPEATING SYLLABLES

Pair with a partner, and turn back to back. One person will recite as clearly as possible, *in any sequence,* any three of the following syllables. The partner will then try to repeat the syllables exactly. Then reverse roles and repeat the exercise.

pee	poo
pih	poo
pay	puh
peh	pur
paa	pi
pah	poi
paw	pyu
po	pow

Do the exercise two or three times; then increase the number of syllables recited to five. As you continue the exercise, increase the speed. You may also try using other initial consonants, such as *k* or *d*, which involve other articulators.

The twenty-five *consonants* of English speech are divided into the *plosives* (made by holding the air momentarily before exploding it outward); the *fricatives* (made by blowing air between the articulators—the tongue, teeth, lips, and hard and soft palates); the *nasals* (made by passing air through the nose); the *glides* (made by moving the tongue); and the *blends* (made by combining other consonants).

Plosive Consonants

t as in tickle, touch, ten

d as in dance, delve, dead

p as in potato, pill, purpose

b as in bombshell, baseball, bed

k as in kick, kindred, collection

g as in giggle, get, go

Fricative Consonants

f as in football, fill, from
v as in voter, veil, vigor
th (unvoiced) as in think, theatre, thrill
th (voiced) as in there, then, they
s as in settle, send, century
z as in zeal, zoo, zebra
sh as in shipshape, shell, sure
zh as in leisure, seizure, azure
h as in hail, high, hiccup

Nasal Consonants

m as in mystery, men, meal
n as in needle, nil, nothing
ng as in sing, song, kingship

Glide Consonants

l as in leader, listen, look
r as in real, rotate, roughhouse
y as in yellow, yesterday, yolk
w as in willow, won't, warrant
wh as in which, whippoorwill, where

Blended Consonants

ch as in chipmunk, choke, child
j as in jump, jail, gentry

Developing crisp, clean consonants helps the actor convey precise meaning and gives the actor's speech a commanding authority. Consonants punctuate speech sound and are crucial in developing the sharpness of an intellectual argument, a witty retort, or a persuasive demand. Consonants are not as susceptible to regional variation as vowels are (an exception is the Cockney *fing* for *thing*) but are, on the other hand, more prone to impediments. The formation of consonants requires rapid and accurate movement of hundreds of muscle systems in the mouth and perfect placement (at the rate of about ten per second) of tongue, teeth, lips, jaw, glottis, gums, and palates (together, these are called the *articulators*). No actor can afford to have flabby, unresponsive, or lazy articulators. Consonant drills, therefore, aim to make an actor's consonants razor sharp.

EXERCISE 14–3
CONSONANTS

Repeat the following consonant drills until you can do them comfortably, rapidly, and, if possible, wittily.

1. Tip it, pippet; tip it, pippet; tip it, pippet.
2. Dab a gak, dab a gak, dab a gak, dab a gak.
3. Azure zoo, azure zoo, azure zoo, azure zoo.
4. Think this fink, think this fink, think this fink.
5. The vase is shaded, the vase is shaded, the vase is shaded.
6. No ming no mong, no ming no mong, no ming no mong.
7. Yell when wending, yell when wending, yell when wending.
8. Jump Chuck, jump Chuck, jump Chuck, jump Chuck.
9. Tapoketa poketa poketa poketa poketa
10. Libid ibid libid ibid libid ibid.
11. Rilly billy dilly killy, rilly billy dilly killy.
12. Potato pit, potato pit, potato pit, potato pit.
13. This is it, this is it, this is it, this is it.
14. Calumny, mercantile, exaggerate, elevate, anglophile.
15. Big a pig gig, big a pig gig, big a pig gig.

EXERCISE 14–4
SPEECHES

When you feel comfortable with the simple drills in Exercise 14–3, try reading the following lines from Shakespeare's *Macbeth.*

Reading aloud, repeat the lines until you can read them clearly and accurately. Note the importance of clear articulation in these speeches.

MACBETH: If it were done when 'tis done, then 'twere well
It were done quickly. If th' assassination
Could trammel up the consequence, and catch
With his surcease, success; that but this blow
Might be the be-all and the end-all—here,
But here, upon this bank and shoal of time,
We'd jump the life to come.

LADY MACBETH: Glamis thou art, and Cawdor, and shalt be
What thou art promised. Yet I do fear thy nature;
It is too full o' th' milk of human kindness
To catch the nearest way. Thou wouldst be great;
Art not without ambition, but without
The illness should attend it. What thou wouldst highly,
That wouldst thou holily; wouldst not play false,
And yet wouldst wrongly win.

No one can say that the speeches in Exercise 14–4 are easy, even for the veteran classical scholar or performer, but you can certainly see that clear articulation is absolutely crucial if any interpretation is to make sense. Only careful speech can distinguish "surcease, success," and "highly . . . holily," and yet these are the sorts of verbal problems with which the actor must deal moment by moment in an articulate play.

For more advanced work in speech and diction, you will want to take special classes or individualized training. But running the vowels and consonants, as in the previous exercises, can help you to understand your own manufacture of phonemes, and to learn how to speak them with clarity and distinction. Speech drills also exercise the articulators and the muscles that move them, giving you a greater capacity to be sharp and subtle with your language, and therefore more powerful in your playing of tactics toward a stage victory. Drilling phonemes also helps give you a confidence toward stage speaking and an ear toward correcting your own impediments or regionalisms—particularly if you can work under the guidance of an interested and qualified teacher.

Summary

Each actor must cultivate the ability to articulate the forty-odd English-language phonemes (speech sounds), for that ability underlies powerful, fluid, subtle, and confident stage speaking and therefore tactical interplay. Mastering the phonemes also is the key to eliminating speech impediments, regional mispronunciations, and speaking timidity. Dramatic improvement in your speaking will come about only with concentrated study under a qualified instructor or coach. Speech drills, however, exercise the articulators and help you gain control of your speaking mechanism.

Using the Voice

Liberation

In the pursuit of victory, in "getting out the VOTE," your voice and speech are the primary tools at your disposal. The voice must be free to coax, to bully, to soothe, to inspire, and to explode. The speech must allow you to articulate, persuade, harangue, dazzle, enchant, and entertain. But voice and speech cannot reach these heights if they are inhibited.

The liberated voice is free from socially bred inhibitions: excessive politeness, timidity, deference, or propriety. The actor's liberation is both psychological and technical. The actor needs confidence that absolutely anything can be said on stage so that breathing and speaking mechanisms will be relaxed and supple enough to make speech vibrant and precise.

Self-consciousness is the inhibitor of speaking. The voices of childhood—yelps, squeals, shouts, silliness, and all—are necessarily channelled during long years of social conditioning into acceptable communicative mechanisms—but at what cost! The average adult voice, perhaps still varied and pungent in the privacy of the shower or the fraternity/sorority drinking party, becomes a timid and wary instrument under the close public scrutiny of a gathering of academic peers. Politeness (the word has the same root as *politics*) is the necessary lubricant for social intercourse, but it stands in the way of vocal and speech development; excessive politeness is the enemy of exciting acting.

The social conditioning we have all passed through (and

continue to pass through) produces a fascinating variety of mis-shapen voices. (Psychiatrists often make their first evaluation of a patient's problem by noting the specific strains in the patient's voice during their first interview.) For young women, there is the classic "little girl voice," a half octave too high, maintained from childhood in an unconscious attempt to remain "Daddy's little girl," or perhaps to avoid competing too directly with a roughhousing older brother. For young men, there is a nasal whine left over from those days when direct confrontation of the parent or teacher was impossible and wheedling was the only way to make an impact.

Sometimes the voices of both sexes suggest that terror under-lies every public statement: that even to say "here" in answer to a roll call may result in a crack on the knuckles for some reason or other. If any of these descriptions seems to fit you, don't worry: *Everybody* experiences, to one degree or another, these vocal shortcomings. There is almost no one whose voice does not "go dead" at one time or another when you suddenly see that everybody is looking at you, or when someone asks you a question you cannot answer, or when you suddenly feel that you're inappropriately dressed. The actor's problem is not worry-ing about a dead or timid voice, but finding the way to coun-teract it, to bring life and energy to the art of speaking.

EXERCISE 15–1

RUDE CHANTS

Chant, as a group:

1. Kill, kill, kill, kill, kill!

2. Barf, barf, barf, barf, barf!

3. Penis, penis, penis, penis, penis!

4. Urine, urine, urine, urine, urine!

In this *impolite* exercise, the point is not to giggle or pretend you're saying something else, but rather to allow your voice the freedom to say, at full volume and with clear speech, the sort of words you don't usually say in public. Try also:

5. Testicle, testicle, testicle, testicle, testicle!

6. Copulate, copulate, copulate, copulate, copulate!

7. Intercourse, intercourse, intercourse, intercourse, intercourse!

8. Masturbate, masturbate, masturbate, masturbate, masturbate!

As an actor, you should be able to say *anything* boldly on stage. No words, no matter how personally odious to you, should simply stick in your throat.

EXERCISE 15–2

RUDE CHEERING

1. Repeat the chants in Exercise 15–1, exploring your pitch range and resonance possibilities. Women: Try to deepen your pitch. Men: Try to enlarge your throat and chest (not nasal) resonance.

2. Chant a "cheer" of "Kill, barf, penis, urine!" Make the cheer *purposeful:* This is the team you are rooting for. Make them win! Make them hear you and know you are cheering them on! Make up gestures and movements for the cheer.

3. Do the same with "Testicle, copulate, intercourse, masturbate!"

This exercise is easy to expand with other words, but keep the doors closed. Your class is a large enough public for this exercise!

Inhibition takes many forms. Another common form is a fear of mispronouncing or misusing large words. In their daily lives, many young people retreat behind a vocabulary of simple language, "fad words," and common clichés simply to avoid the possibility of making a mistake. (And how terrified we were, as adolescents, of making a mistake!) Therefore the language they bring to acting is essentially slovenly, immature, and bland. In the theatre, of course, language is created by playwrights, but most young actors have initial (and sometimes continuing) difficulties in rising to the language of the play. Often they consciously or unconsciously rewrite the script into their own words; more often they stumble and mutter over any four-syllable words they find in the text. You can lick this problem. An actor must love words and word play. While it is true that many dramatic characters are inarticulate (particularly in plays from the 1950s), a great many more are not; each actor must rise to the level of verbal dexterity that the character has achieved—and often the characters are verbal dynamos.

EXERCISE 15–3

FANCY TALK

Separately, and after checking the meaning and pronunciation of words unfamiliar to you, say to someone (real or imaginary) with a good deal of *fun:*

1. Throckmorton's in an anomalous predicament!
2. I detest John's egregious braggadocio!
3. What a stentorian denunciation!
4. Her perfidious egalitarianism is obnoxious!
5. Thwart Ellen's obstinacy!
6. Could you correlate the data mellifluously?
7. Long live ubiquitous serendipity!
8. Disambiguate your metaphor!
9. Come to the Christmas colloquium.
10. Restrain your ribald riposting!
11. Cease your antediluvian antics!
12. Your libidinous delusions are tantalizing!
13. I adore elocutionary magnificence!
14. Startling complexities abound!
15. Beware the inevitable consequences!
16. Facilitate copulation!
17. Barf before pontificating!

The last two sentences combine Exercises 15–1 and 15–3. Make up additional combinations of long words and "rude" words and speak them freely in all ranges of your voice. Examples of speeches to say to a (real or imaginary) partner:

1. "I fart at thee!" (Ben Jonson, *The Alchemist*)
2. "The bawdy hand of time is on the prick of noon." (Shakespeare, *Romeo and Juliet*)

3. "Extraordinary how potent cheap music is." (Noel Coward, *Private Lives*)

4. "WEE! WAA! WONDERFUL! I'm stiff! Stiff in the wind! My mane, stiff in the wind! My flanks! My hooves! Mane on my legs, on my flanks, like whips! Raw! Raw! *I'm raw! Raw!*" (Peter Schaffer, *Equus*)

5. "Come down outa dere, yuh yellow, brass-buttoned, Belfast bum, yuh! Come down and I'll knock yer brains out! Yuh lousy, stinkin' yellow mutt of a Catholic-moiderin' bastard!" (Eugene O'Neill, *The Hairy Ape*)

6. "Oh, I should think I was poor and had nothing to bestow if I were reduced to an inglorious ease and freed from the agreeable fatigues of solicitation." (William Congreve, *The Way of the World*)

7. "You see, you piss better when I'm not there." (Samuel Beckett, *Waiting for Godot*)

8. "Detested kite! Thou liest." (Shakespeare, *King Lear*)

9. "I'm a bad publisher because I hate books. Or to be more precise, prose. Or to be even more precise, modern prose, I mean modern novels, first novels and second novels, all that promise and sensibility it falls upon me to judge, to put the firm's money on, and then to push for the third novel, see it done, see the dust jacket done, see the dinner for the national literary editors done, see the signing in Hatchards done, see the lucky author cook himself to death, all in the name of literature. You know what you and Emma have in common? You love literature. I mean you love modern prose literature, I mean you love the new novel by the new Casey or Spinks. It gives you both a thrill." (Harold Pinter, *Betrayal*)

EXERCISE 15–4

ADDRESS A GROUP

Thus far you have spoken your lines to a single (real or imaginary) partner. Now address an imaginary group. Using the fanciful sentences, rude chants, and dramatic texts in the previous exercises, deliver them to:

1. A college class

2. A kindergarten class

3. A bar full of people

4. An army battalion

5. A sorority luncheon

6. Your family

Enlarging the audience to your remarks draws forth more vocal power and articulation and makes you use "more voice" than you need when you are simply addressing an intimate friend. Addressing people who are noisy, deaf, deranged, hostile, or unintelligent can add verbal force and articulate distinction to your speech. Practice enlarging your audience for larger speeches, perhaps by assuming that your character wants to be overheard by others in an adjacent room. This technique can bring your voice and speech to necessary stage levels without sacrificing the directness or honesty of your delivery.

Purposefulness

Purposefulness is what ties the liberated voice to the actor's approach. For the actor's voice and speech are not developed as ends in themselves; an instrument, after all, is only useful while you use it. Basically, the actor's speaking mechanism is the prime weapon of the character's tactical pursuits—the prime implement for "getting out the VOTE."

In the theatre, as in life, people should speak not because they have to but because they *want* to. Every word you speak on stage must be (and seem to be) directed toward your victory; every word must have some tactical service to your cause. As a character, you should not appear to speak simply because the author put words in your mouth, but because you have desires, plans, objectives—and because speaking out is the way you expect to get them! Every word spoken onstage, therefore, must be spoken with purposefulness: Words must come from human desire, not mechanical necessity. This purpose, above all else, brings compelling power to your vocal instrument.

Some examples illustrate how purposefulness affects the way you use your voice:

You are at a football game as guest of a friend. The people

around you cheer. You do not care who wins the game, but you cheer because you're supposed to.

You are at a football game rooting for your team, for people with whom you identify. You cheer. Your cheers are more vigorous; your voice is fuller and more intense. Why? Because you *care*. Because you are using your voice to try to help your team. You have a *purpose*.

You are instructed to say, as distinctly as possible, "Pull up on the door handle." You do so.

Your two-year-old sister is crying in a locked car; nearby a building is on fire. You tell her, "Pull up on the door handle!" You are more distinct, your speech is clearer, more demanding, more penetrating. Why?

Good stage speech results from allying purpose with a liberated and versatile vocal mechanism. It is not sufficient to have a good voice; the actor must *want* to vocalize, and must want to demand, cajole, attract, or compel others with the voice as a primary instrument. Even the simplest and most technical vocal exercise—"bah bah bah bah bah," for example—can be enhanced by giving the exercise an interpersonal purpose (to calm someone's nerves, to amuse someone, to solicit someone's sympathy). When your purpose is strong enough, it will override any shyness or timidity or inhibitions you might have. Utterly mild and noncommunicative persons can break through giant psychological sound barriers when they see someone stealing their car, or kissing their sweetheart, or running the wrong way with the football. Create, in your mind, a sufficient victory, and energize your voice and speech in its pursuit.

EXERCISE 15–5
Adding Purpose

Go back to Exercise 13–4. Using the same speeches, create a strong situational victory for each speech, and speak the words purposefully to a (real or imaginary) partner.

Summary

The actor's voice and stage speech are to be *used*, not merely exhibited. To this end they must be free from inhibiting factors, particularly shyness, excessive politeness, and fear of making verbal mistakes. The actor should develop confidence in his or her verbal dexterity, should become comfortable with both rude language and intricate linguistic construction. *Purpose*, finally, is the motive force of good stage speaking; the actor must ally his or her voice and speaking mechanism with a will to achieve victory in a dramatic situation.

The Actor's Body

Agility

Body training for the actor follows many separate paths. Perhaps surprisingly, *developing strength and stamina* is first on the list. One doesn't always associate athletic functions with artistic endeavors, but the sheer physical work of the actor is often gruelling. After all, the demands of the role may involve several hours of onstage time, running up and down stairs, fighting, duelling, changing costume, *with maximum physical control*. Mere enthusiasm will not accomplish this control. Such famous actors as Laurence Olivier and Jane Fonda are well known for their demanding physical regimens, developed as a result of their acting careers. Body building, aerobic exercise, and competitive athletics are now routine activities for actors of all ages.

Develop dexterity and coordination. "Learn your lines and don't bump into the scenery" is the traditional "first lesson" of acting. Physical dexterity means more than merely not bumping into the scenery, however, and more than being able to speak and move at the same time. The actor who is physically coordinated—who can move *with precision and passion at the same time*—can convey meaningful behavior with far more complexity than the actor who merely speaks the words trippingly on the tongue.

Develop physical dynamics. Dynamics means physical force in action. The actor is always either in action or *potentially* in action, always moving or on the verge of moving. An actor who seems just about to hit out, kiss someone, explode, or bolt away is an exciting, dynamic actor. The body can be trained toward this dynamic, supple, physical readiness.

Develop specific movement skills. Finally, actor training involves the learning of specific physical patterns, such as ballet, ballroom dancing, period dancing, fencing, hand-to-hand combat, mime, gesture, martial arts, period movement, and circus technique. These skills are often useful in themselves, and they increase the actor's physical versatility, confidence, and poise. Additionally, they aid an actor's sense of timing and physical aesthetics. Indeed, the relationship between acting and dance has been intimate since the dramas of ancient Greece. Many actor-training programs begin with dance, mime, and stage movement.

Exercise 16–1 gets the blood moving, loosens and stretches the ligaments, flexes several hundred muscles, and makes you feel good. It is *only* a warm-up, however. After fifteen minutes of sitting in a classroom chair, you're back where you started. Therefore actors need to know how to warm up fast and effectively, for they will do it often.

EXERCISE 16–1

FAST WARM-UP

Stand with feet comfortably apart, hands on hips. Swing the torso to the right, stretch, hold. Swing the torso to the left, stretch, hold, Repeat.

Repeat, extending the leading arm.

Repeat, extending both arms.

Return to front, arms at sides. Bend over, touching the floor with the fingers, bending the knees as necessary.

Tap the floor with the fingers. Make a rhythm of tapping on the floor. Add the fingernails to the tapping. Add the palms.

Rise up slowly, uncurling the spine vertebra by vertebra.

Extend the head upward without straining, allowing it to "float" freely atop the spinal column.

Rotate the head in leftward and rightward spirals, each time spiralling in to a relaxed "floating" position atop the spine.

Rotate the arms in large circles, then in smaller circles, first together and then one at a time. Reverse the direction of the circles.

Swing the legs from the hip joints.

Bounce ten times, arms at your sides.

Bounce ten times, arms akimbo.
Run in place.

Alignment

The proper alignment of the body—all vital organs poised in a balanced relationship to maximize their healthy functioning—was the primary goal of F. Matthias Alexander, whose Alexander technique is the best-known and most effective alignment system for actors. The basic Alexander alignment is a standing position with

1. The head "floating" easily atop the spine
2. The neck free and relaxed
3. The shoulders spread out (not back)
4. The torso lengthened and widened; the rib cage expanded; the vertebrae separated, not crunched together
5. The pelvis freely rotating, the hip joints free and rolling

The Alexander technique produces not a specific posture but an inner alignment of bodily organs. It promotes good posture, but it also promotes relaxed breathing, deep resonance, clear speech, and coordinated whole-body movement. Alexander adherents also add health, longevity, improved appearance, and enhanced self-image to this list.

The Alexander alignment "works" because it gives the lungs room to function; it reduces constriction in the throat and mouth; and it gives the diaphragm enough pelvic support to provide a basis of sustained full breathing. The body is "poised" so that movement springs quite naturally from every limb or digit, or from the trunk itself. Compare this with the hunched-over position of most adults at work or watching television!

The following exercises are necessarily introductory. Enthusiasts of the physical training methods described below devote lifetimes to the study of the various potentials of the human mechanism. But all the exercises suggest ways in which the actor can begin physical self-exploration and self-training to develop greater strength, stamina, dexterity, coordination, and physical dynamics.

EXERCISE 16–2

IMPROVING ALIGNMENT

Stand on the floor, legs comfortably apart. Hunch your shoulders down, squeeze your head down onto your neck, lock your knees, clench your fists, and say, "Hah hah hah hah hah." The sound will be *terrible.* Now try this:

Relax your arms, open your fists, swing your arms lightly, and let your head "float" upwards, keeping your chin level.

Rotate your head one or two times each way, ending in a spiral and "floating" your head as high as you can without straining.

Flex your knees slightly and rotate your hips, coming to rest in a balanced position.

Broaden your shoulders straight out, left and right, and open your rib cage, raising and expanding your ribs outward, forward, and upward. [Imagine a gentle tug from two wires attached to your ribs three inches below your nipples, each pulling upward at a 45-degree angle forward and outward.]

Lengthen your spine without locking it. Say, "Hah hah hah hah hah."

Twist your torso freely; walk and turn and reach while maintaining this alignment. Say, "Hah hah hah hah hah."

Exercise 16–2 will have an immediate short-term result: You will notice greater resonance and more unfettered breathing right away. It is not a simple matter to make this improved alignment a part of your unconscious daily movements, however, nor is it a simple thing to sustain the alignment—at first—without feeling stiff and awkward. Good internal alignment takes a great deal of practice and concentration: You are changing habits of a lifetime, and you cannot expect to do that easily or quickly. But the end result will be greater physical and vocal presence and ability.

Velocity: Accelerating, Decelerating, and Constant

The ability to control acceleration and deceleration is crucial in developing physical dexterity and in creating the dynamics of movement. Accelerating and decelerating movements make clear that you are thinking while moving, that your mind is generating the movements you make. Constant velocity movements, on the other hand, indicate that you are simply executing movements generated by someone else—the director, for example.

Constant velocity movements figure in the portrayal of characters "trying to get a grip on themselves," such as a reformed drug addict putting down the bottle of pills. But for the beginning actor, constant velocity movement usually shows that the actor is moving only because he or she has to—or is supposed to—and not because he or she *wants* to. This is invariably a serious flaw.

EXERCISE 16–3
ACCELERATION/DECELERATION

1. Stand, extend your arms outward, palms front, elbows slightly flexed.
2. Now bring your palms together in a clap, moving your arms at a *constant rate of speed.*
3. Now clap at a *constantly accelerating* rate of speed.
4. Now clap at a *constantly decelerating* rate of speed.

Notice the characteristics of the three claps. The first (constant rate of speed) is like perfunctory applause. The second is a gesture of victory—"Eureka!" The third is like bringing the hands together in prayer.

Practice constant, accelerating, and decelerating motions while repeating each of these actions five times:

1. Putting your hand down on a table
2. Moving your hand toward—and seizing—a prop revolver your partner is holding
3. Turning to look at someone behind you
4. Punching a pillow
5. Getting out of a chair
6. Walking to a predetermined spot on the floor
7. Sitting down
8. Lifting a drink (shot-glass size) to your lips and drinking it
9. Touching your partner's neck

10. Touching your partner's hair

11. Taking off your sweater

12. Putting a bottle of pills on a table

13. Lying down on a sofa

14. Pointing your finger at someone; pointing at some *part* of some-
    one

Accelerating motions tend to be exciting and enthusiastic. Decelerating motions tend to be graceful and gentle. Constant motions tend to be bored and dutiful. Guess which kinds are most useful in acting. And guess which kinds you most often see with beginning actors!

Counterpoise

Contraposto is an Italian word, used mainly in the analysis of paintings and sculptures, describing counterpoised physical positions in which the body is twisted so that the shoulders and the hips, the arms and the legs, are in different planes. Michelangelo's paintings and sculptures, which are known for their contraposto, are especially illuminating for actors.

The counterpoised body is both dynamic and balanced; it can be coiled for action even though it seems to be at rest. By contrast, the standing-at-attention, squared off body—a product of "stand-up-straight" discipline rather than actor training—is static and uninteresting on stage and is impossible to mobilize emotionally or physically.

EXERCISE 16–4

CONTRAPOSTO

1. Feet planted comfortably on the floor, the body aligned as in Exercise 16–2, turn the hips ninety degrees to the left.

2. Extend the right arm up and away. Turn the head another ninety degrees left. Flex the knees.

3. Spring to the reverse position.

4. Relax.

5. Walk, with a decelerating velocity, to a point ten yards away, turning as you come to a halt.

6. Walk, with a decelerating velocity, to a chair ten yards away; turn and coil as you sit.

7. Toss your head one way, then another.

8. Look one way and point another. Reverse.

9. Get a good sturdy sofa away from a wall. Using the sofa's seat, arms, and back, find ten physically dynamic *contraposto* positions for yourself, moving from one to the other in a fluid acceleration/deceleration movement. Play a scene or improvisation with someone, moving around the sofa in this fashion.

The body contracts on itself for protection. It extends outward for expression and sometimes for attack. The magnitude of contractions and extensions is one signification of an actor's physical freedom: Children, for example, are usually quite uninhibited in extensions; adults are far more often restrained.

EXERCISE 16–5

CONTRACTION/EXTENSION

1. To the sounds of a drumbeat, or a command, CONTRACT! ... CONTRACT! ... CONTRACT! ... CONTRACT!

2. To the sounds of a drumbeat, or a command, EXTEND! ... EXTEND! ... EXTEND! ... EXTEND! ... LEAP UP! ... LEAP UP! ... CONTRACT!

3. Walk with a decelerating speed and roll into a tight spiral, knotting yourself up into a little ball. Hold for ten seconds, compressing and compressing, and then EXPLODE!

4. Respond to an imaginary:

Punch in the stomach

Fire in the seat of your pants

Heart attack

Shout to surrender

Cry for help

Summary

The actor's body must be trained into a supple, strong, energetic, dexterous, and dynamic instrument. Physical training programs, which may take years, involve the learning of precise movement skills, such as mime and formal dance, but some simple exercises can start you immediately on the road to establishing good physical alignment, control over the direction and velocity (acceleration and deceleration) of physical movements, dynamic counterpoise and balance, and the potential for bold (explosive) physical movement.

Voice and Body Integration

Coordination

The integration of voice and body—"being able to speak and move at the same time"—is the acid test of the actor's instrument. Master this and you will progress accordingly. Fail and you must go back and try again.

In life we move and speak at the same time without thinking; in the theatre, however, we are required to think: to learn lines written by an author and movements initiated by a director. To reproduce these unselfconsciously isn't easy. Concentrating on our lines, we may stiffen physically; concentrating on our movement, we may let our dialog come out stilted and mechanical. The fluidity of speech and motion, common enough in our everyday existence, is easily lost through the divided consciousness of acting.

Concentration on the character's victory, and on the tactics of expectations necessary to gain that victory, through or with the other persons in the play, will integrate the actor's mind. Thus pursuing the VOTE principles will pull together the liberated instrument and make it compelling.

Once developed, the actor's instrument can be used only when it is forgotten. While playing a concerto, the violinist is not thinking about strings and bows and frets; the violinist is thinking about making music. Likewise, in playing the role, the actor is not thinking of phonemes or decelerations; he or she is thinking of victories and how to achieve them quickly. Finally, the actor becomes an instrument.

Developing good voice-body integration, or coordination, demands that you are quite clear about what you want in a scene, and that you are entirely free to put your whole body (voice and movement) into your quest for victory. If the concentration on victory is your mainspring, both voice and body will serve that concentration: They will be integrated by the strength of your commitment to get what you want.

The following exercise should be a useful first step in integrating voice and body.

EXERCISE 17–1

COMMANDS

1. Try to make a (real or imaginary) partner come to a specific spot by walking five steps to the spot while saying, "Come right here!" As you reach the spot, pivot around and point to the floor. The movement and speaking should be simultaneous, and you should pivot and point while you are still speaking. Experiment with various timings of this.

2. Do this exercise with these alternate lines:
   a. I want you to come right here, please.
   b. Listen, George, I think it's very important that you come right here before I get any angrier than I already am.
   c. Come, friend. [Or: Come, my darling.]

3. Do this exercise while walking to a sofa, or to one of two adjacent chairs, turning and sitting during your last line. Choose lines from 1 and 2 above, or write new lines. [But write, don't improvise.]

You should be able to ally short lines with long moves, and long lines with short moves, and, in fact, to time out any combination of movement and speech in an effective, relaxed, confident manner. Work also on completing your movements with a decelerating turn or sit synchonized with your last word.

EXERCISE 17–2

SPEECHES WITH BUSINESS

Study and memorize one of the following speeches—all of which are taken from the opening scenes of plays. Or memorize a short speech from the first few pages of any play of your choice. From the context, imagine whom you are speaking to, and use your imagination to create a VOTE approach to the speech. Rehearse the speech privately until you feel confident of the lines.

1. "Since the Professor and his wife came to live here, life is off the track. . . . I sleep at odd hours, for lunch and dinner I eat a lot of highly spiced dishes, drink wine . . . all that is not good for your health. We never used to have a free minute. Sonia and I worked— I can tell you that—and now it's only Sonia who works, and I sleep, eat, drink. . . . There's no good in it." (Anton Chekhov, *Uncle Vanya*]

2. "We've been in rehearsal four days. Due to a technical fluke with the contract—not your fault, of course—Mr. Billy Hertz, our leading man, is on his way to Hollywood and a flowery two-picture deal. As of today, here and now, we are minus a leading man. Since we are booked into Boston on the 28th, we are in trouble!" [Clifford Odets, *The Country Girl*]

3. "Honey, don't push with your fingers. If you have to push with something, the thing to push with is a crust of bread. And chew—chew! Animals have sections in their stomachs which enable them to digest food without mastication, but human beings are supposed to chew their food before they swallow it down. Eat food leisurely, son, and really enjoy it. A well-cooked meal has lots of delicate flavors that have to be held in the mouth for appreciation. So chew your food and give your salivary glands a chance to function!" [Tennessee Williams, *The Glass Menagerie*]

4. "The street is lined with cars. There's not a breath of fresh air in the neighborhood. The grass don't grow any more, you can't raise a carrot in the back yard. They should've had a law against apartment houses. Remember those two beautiful elm trees out there? When I and Biff hung the swing between them? . . . They should've

arrested the builder for cutting those down. They massacred the neighborhood." [Arthur Miller, *Death of a Salesman*]

Now, with the speech learned, practice "delivering" it to a (real or imaginary) partner, *using real props*—or substitute props—and performing one of the following pieces of stage business at the same time:

1. Changing your clothing
2. Mixing and drinking a Manhattan cocktail
3. Filling, lighting, and puffing on a pipe
4. Mixing, dressing, and tasting a fruit salad
5. Shuffling a deck of cards and dealing out two hands of gin rummy
6. Peeling and eating a banana, then disposing of the peel

It is, of course, necessary to have the business well in hand. You must, for example, know how to mix a Manhattan cocktail. The behavior must be familiar; for example, don't smoke a pipe unless you customarily smoke one.* Choose other business, if you like, but choose business that is progressive (not simply repetitive) and sufficiently complex so that it involves several parts of your body.

You will probably find that Exercise 17–2 requires a good deal of practice. You will quickly find that there are literally thousands of ways in which your lines and business may be coordinated. How does the behavior affect the speech? How do the speech and the feelings that come with it affect the behavior? Don't try to "interpret" the speech according to the context of the play; treat the speech simply as an isolated exercise, and let the speech create behavior that supports your "delivery." Can you combine certain behaviors with the language so as to charm your partner? To threaten him or her? To beg for pity? To subvert? To frighten? To overwhelm?

---

*It is the opinion of the author that no student actor who is not already a confirmed smoker should ever be asked—or allowed—to smoke as part of an acting assignment.

EXERCISE 17-3

PHYSICAL PUNCTUATION

Select any speech that you have memorized, possibly the one from the previous exercise, and deliver it to a (real or imaginary) partner while doing a repetitive physical action, such as

1. Jogging in place

2. Skipping rope

3. Beating egg yolks

4. Doing sit-ups

5. Combing your hair

6. Playing the piano

7. Dribbling a (pretend) basketball

8. Shaving

Talk "over" the physical action; make yourself understood—and your intentions felt—over and above the distraction of your movement.

Now "punctuate" the speech by stopping your movement at a certain point in the text. Experiment with several possible moments. Experiment with stopping one movement—and later in the speech starting another one.

You are your own best teacher of what "works" in Exercise 17–3. Much of the director's work in staging a play is finding the right physical punctuation to drive home significant emotional transitions. You can anticipate this work in your acting by finding out how a change of physical rhythm coordinates with a change in the plot, or in a character's intention or understanding of a relationship.

EXERCISE 17-4

PHYSICAL RHYTHMS

Memorize one or more of the one-line speeches in Exercise 15–3. Deliver each speech to a (real or imaginary) partner together with an accelerating movement of your hand, such as pointing or slamming your fist on a table.

Deliver each speech with a decelerating movement, such as sitting in a chair, crossing the room and turning, or touching your partner.

EXERCISE 17–5

VERBAL RHYTHMS

Give each of the following commands with an accelerating tempo, then with a decelerating tempo.

1. "Get out of this room."

2. "Give me that!"

3. "Go out there and win!"

4. "Kiss me before I explode."

5. "To be or not to be, that is the question."

Combine the accelerating tempo with an accelerating arm/hand movement. Combine the decelerating tempo with a decelerating physical movement.

Tempo

The ability to experiment with tempos—both physical and verbal—is an acting asset. There are no intrinsically "right" or "wrong" tempos in the theatre, and rarely do tempos simply accelerate or decelerate in straight-line fashion; but a rhythmic variety is characteristic both of fine acting and of life itself. The beginning actor is often stuck in a repetitive, plodding rhythm, which is neither dramatic nor lifelike, but rather a product of stage fright and dutiful "line reading."

How do the varying rhythms in Exercise 17–5 affect your feelings? Your interaction with your partner? Ask your partner—if you have one—what impact your accelerated deliveries had on him or her, or your decelerated deliveries. Get comfortable with this exercise by repeating it several times, varying your text, intention, rhythm, and acting partner.

EXERCISE 17–6

SPEECH/MOVEMENT TIMING

Select a one-minute speech from any play—such as the speeches at the beginning of this chapter (p. 135). Analyze the VOTE for the character in that speech. Plot out a series of actions that coordinate with the speech, such as crossing the stage, walking around a sofa, picking up a book and tossing it aside, sitting down, smiling, tossing your head, and crossing your legs. Define where the other characters are located. Rehearse the speech very carefully so that you can time the actions to specific words. Create a pattern of accelerating and decelerating movements and verbal tempos. Create two or three punctuations. Let the speech climax at the end, so that the crossing of the legs becomes a *significant* action concluding your line of thought.

When you can do this *unconsciously*, you will have taken a very long stride toward becoming an actor.

The Handicapped Actor

The emphasis on voice and body-movement in actor training should not obscure the fact that some actors are handicapped in one or the other capacity. There are very fine actors who cannot hear or speak: Witness the Theatre of the Deaf. And there are excellent actors who are paraplegics and amputees. There is certainly nothing superhuman about most actors' instruments, and some indeed transcend serious limitations. Acting is a portrayal of human life and the human condition, and anyone who has a sense of that, and can portray a goodly fraction of it, will find the opportunity to do so. But voice-body integration—the integration of such capacities as the actor has and can nourish—is a critical step in every actor's development, for only through such integration can an actor maximize his or her potential.

Summary

Concentration on victory and on the VOTE of the character integrates the voice and body components of the actor's instrument. Moving and speaking simultaneously and unselfconsciously is difficult for actors to master, but it must be learned if acting is to be fluid, rhythmically dynamic, energetic, lifelike, and properly punctuated. Each actor may have limitations or handicaps, but developing the acting instrument means integrating, as much as possible, all your capacities for effectively dramatic speech and movement.

Imagination and Discipline

Fantasy

Imagination (fantasy, creativity, inspiration) is the wellspring of the acting impulse. Discipline (responsibility, punctuality, soundness) shapes actors into an ensemble of collaborative creation. Without either, fine acting cannot exist; therefore both imagination and discipline must be developed and integrated in the actor's personality.

Imagination is the source of the actor's victory, the source of purpose and intention. Romeo wants to marry Juliet, and that is the victory the actor pursues. But how does the actor pursue it? Not simply through clinical observation or rational depiction. "I want to marry Juliet" is a lively, compelling, intense fantasy. It obviously has deeply sexual origins. It may also engage fantasies of worship, adventure, social acceptance, class revenge, and fetishism, as well as fantasies of annihilation, damnation, gluttony, domination, and isolation. The most exciting Romeo is clearly the one whose fantasies are the liveliest, most provocative, most insistent, and most enchanting. The actor who is simply pursuing a marriage certificate will be a pedestrian Romeo, no matter how brilliantly he reads Romeo's lines.

When approaching a part, the actor quickly comes to grips with the character's major victories and intentions. Research into the part, into the period of the play, and into the psychology of the character can further define the character's victories. But defining victories is only the first step in playing them. One still must bring them to life; and here *your* life—the life of your mind—plays a crucial role.

The imagination is a rich, unfettered world where anything can happen, where lust, torture, bestiality, suicide, and apocalyptic experiences of indescribable dimensions all have their place. These private places are rarely shared even in the most intimate relationships. Some private places are securely locked away: At times we refuse to admit, even to ourselves, that we have such thoughts. (Such locking away, called *repression*, is often the cause of serious neurotic disorders.) Often our secret fantasies are so unsettling, in our conscious contemplation of them, that they come to the fore only in our dreams and nightmares. Certainly the theatre has been one of society's great inventions for dealing with this private world of the imagination: The continuing uproar over the predominance of "sex and violence" on television does not obscure the fact that the theatre, at its deepest level, is about little else.

As an actor must be uninhibited vocally and physically, so he or she must be uninhibited in the imaginative life. We not only want to see Romeo "want to marry" Juliet, we want to see him *tremble* at the sight of her. We want to see her struggle to catch her breath when she sees him for the first time. We want to see the blood rush up in their cheeks; we want to see their lips quiver. We also want to see their absolute *terror* of saying the wrong thing. In short, we (in the audience) want to see the actors experience all the rapture, confusion, and anxiety of the profoundest first love there ever was! This occurs in the voice and body—but in the mind as well. Indeed, the mind is confronting the body, and the fantasies of the mind are straining against the limitations of the physical being.

Self-Exploration

The actor's imagination—the actor's fantasies and fears—are often well submerged, frequently all but inaccessible. Imagination exercises can help the actor probe his or her own unconscious, inducing a "daydream" state where the emotions, memories, and longings commingle just below the surface. These exercises in self-exploration are akin to hypnosis and meditation

—both of which are often used by actors to attain what Stanislavski called the "creative mood."

EXERCISE 18–1

COLD/HOT

For this exercise you need a group leader or instructor and a dimmer to control lighting in the room.

Lie or sit on the floor. As the light brightens, imagine that the temperature gets warmer, then hotter, then uncomfortably hot, then *painfully* hot.

Imagine that by chanting 'ohhhhhhhhhhh," you and the others can appease the "gods" that control the temperature.

As the light fades, imagine that the temperature cools, that it gets cold and then freezing.

Imagine that you are dying.

Imagine that by chanting "eeeeeeeeeeeee," the group can appease the "gods" and restore warmth to the world. Imagine that rhythmic stamping reinforces the chant.

The group leader may improvise additional variants for you to imagine.

EXERCISE 18–2

AGE REGRESSION/ADVANCEMENT

Look at a partner; study him or her well. Feel your partner's face with your hand. Imagine your partner at half his or her age. At half again that age. Imagine your partner as four years old. As two years old. As a naked infant. As a naked adolescent. REALIZE THAT YOUR PARTNER *WAS* A NAKED ADOLESCENT.

Imagine your partner at double his or her age. At age eighty-five. Look beneath your partner's skin at the skull. Feel your partner's skull. Imagine your partner dead, lying in a shallow grave. Imagine your partner as a skeleton. REALIZE THAT YOUR PARTNER *WILL* BECOME A SKELETON.

Back away from your partner so that several yards separate you. Envision your partner's birth-to-death cycle. Imagine, in fantasy, relationships between your partner and persons in your family, or persons close to you, or you yourself at different ages.

On signal, approach and hug your partner.
The group leader may improvise additional variants for your imagination.

Fantasy is most effective as an individual exercise, not a class exercise. Fantasizing sexual or violent relationships, for example, may be embarrassing when "performed" at an instructor's command; if given free play within an acting scene, however, such fantasizing can give life to the most pedestrian stage relationship. You are always the master of your own imagination. When you are freed from inhibition and from worry over remembering your lines, your imagination can give your stage character as much sensitivity and liveliness as you experience in your own dream/nightmare world.

Emotional Recall

Konstantin Stanislavski developed and made famous the acting technique called "emotional recall." Simply put, this is a technique by which the actor, in order to stimulate emotions for a given scene, recalls from memory an emotion-laden personal experience of his or her own life. No other acting technique has generated as much controversy in the twentieth century as this one. Stanislavski eventually abandoned it, and few acting teachers today recommend it, because it forces actors to "hype themselves up" with stimuli unrelated to the dramatic material at hand.

But emotional recall may quite usefully come into play in comparing your "acted" scenes to your "lived" ones. When you played the scene of an argument with your (stage) father, did you get as angry as when you argued with your real father? Is your stage love scene as passionate as your high school crush was? If your stage emotions fall short of your real-life peak experiences, your imagination and fantasy are not working for your character as well as they worked for you. It may be useful to imagine that your stage father is your real father (at that time in your life) and that your stage lover is your high school sweetheart, if that stimulates your imagination and enriches your fantasy about your partner.

Discipline

Discipline is the flip side of imagination. It is the final element in an actor's instrument, and the one that should be taken for granted by the time an actor begins serious study.

Unlike most of the creative arts, acting is a team enterprise; an actor is, by necessity, a team player. Rehearsals, although frequently improvisational, freewheeling, and fun, are serious artistic collaborations. Absolutely faithful attendance and punctuality are universally required.

The discipline of the actor is what permits the shared trust of the ensemble. If the imagination is to be free and the fantasy uninhibited, then each actor must feel the support of the whole and must know that the trust will not be misplaced, the fantasy not misread, and the emotions not ridiculed. An atmosphere of trust permits the wildest leaps of imagination and the most daring personal choices.

The theatre is always greater than the sum of its parts. Acting excels only inasmuch as *interacting* excels. To be on time, to learn your lines on time, to commit to the reality of the situation and style, to treat the work seriously and with spirit—these are the marks of the disciplined actor and the joys of the disciplined acting company. *There is no better place to learn discipline than acting class.* People do not work one way in school and another in the professional world; discipline is an artistic habit, and it has its own artistic rewards. It is not merely something you have to accept; if you are a serious actor, you accept it because you *want* to.

There are, obviously, no "discipline exercises." Show up on time, lines learned, ready to go, and commit yourself. Do your homework. Experiment. Share with your co-workers. And do it every day of your life. That's discipline—starting now.

Summary

Imagination and discipline are the intangible aspects of an actor's instrument—intangible because they are attitudes rather than skills. The actor's imagination must be liberal, provocative, and lively; the actor's self-discipline must be firm, unambiguous, and freely given. Imagination and discipline can be practiced, perhaps even taught, but they are intrinsic aspects of every committed artist in the theatre. They should come into play *now*, not at some vague future in your studies or career.

PART FOUR

THE ACTOR'S TECHNIQUE

Technique is a word most American actors regard with mixed feelings. On the plus side, technique is simply what distinguishes fine artists or craftspersons in any field. On the minus side, an empty technique—technical ability without feeling or person-to-person interplay—is a shallow approximation of acting, bearing little resemblance to the real thing.

The actor's technique should be part of the entire acting experience, not a final gloss or "finesse" added at the last phase of rehearsal. Technique, indeed, is part of life itself; it helps us achieve victories in life, as well as on the stage. Most of what we know as acting technique is simply effective human behavior: actions that are more economical, gestures that are more pointed, speeches that are more precise and more intense than ineffective ones. Learning to be a more technically proficient actor is also learning to be a more effective person-to-person communicator in daily life.

No element of acting technique is ever wholly artificial or solely theatrical. Even extremely non-naturalistic technique, such as may be found in the Japanese Noh or Kabuki drama, for example, is based on true feeling and effective action toward some sort of victory. Thus every "technical" instruction in Part Four must be regarded as an extension of the life and

147

personality of your character and must be understood in terms
of the human reality of your character's situation and VOTE
breakdown.

Phrasing

Diction

Diction, emphasis, and inflection are three overlapping aspects of the actor's ability to speak the lines of the text. Together they comprise phrasing.

It goes without saying that the actor should be able to speak words clearly and with meaning. Beyond that, the actor may choose a manner of phrasing and pronunciation (diction), point out the importance of specific words in the text (emphasis), and suggest unusual interpretation or provoke a specific response by a particular intonation (inflection). Hamlet's first line, "A little more than kin, and less than kind," is virtually meaningless without careful diction, precise emphasis (on *kin* and *kind*), and sarcastic inflection.

Diction—the manner in which words are enunciated and put together—demands the actor's greatest attention to the clarity of the dramatic text and to the clear expression of the character's tactical pursuits. Diction does not require that you continually overpronounce, but that your enunciation serves the character and the script, and is developed as far as your skill and the dramatic situation permit.

Good diction requires absolute comprehension of the meaning of your words and of the syntax that holds them together. Then it requires tying the words to the VOTE, specifically to the tactics that the words represent. Are you asking a question?

Are you silencing an opponent? Are you begging for approval? Are you trying to get the last word? Are you trying to provoke an argument? All of these—and many more—are verbal tactics that require complete control of your diction.

Diction requires both understanding (of the character, of the situation, of the VOTE) and a well-trained vocal instrument. It also requires concentration on this question: "What do I want the other character to hear and understand?" This question, more than any other single thought, will focus your diction and give it a dramatic—and dynamic—sense of direction. Since a play is a fixed document, and since the other actor has read and heard your lines several times, you must work to make the other character (your acting partner) hear your words freshly, as if for the first time. The end product of diction is not what is said, but what is heard. If you can make the other actors hear and understand you, the audience will hear and understand you.

Young actors often deliberately muddle their diction to demonstrate emotional involvement. This tactic is not only undramatic, it is unlifelike. Listen to people in a heated discussion: As they get angrier, their diction actually *improves.* They grow clearer, more lucid, sometimes even eloquent. They are trying to *win* their argument; they want to win a victory, not merely to indicate anger. Listen to a parent speaking to a disobedient child; a schoolteacher speaking to a group of unruly students; a bartender speaking to a crowd of rowdy drinkers. Inevitably the more difficult and taxing the situation, the more powerful and precise the diction. Penetrating diction is one of the most potent tools the actor can lend to his or her character. Your instrument must be honed—and your approach focused—to deliver good diction at all times.

Good diction enables the audience to understand the play. If the actor cannot distinguish between "I ask you" and "I asked you," a moment in the play will surely suffer. After several such moments, the audience's attention will surely drift. While the audience puzzles as to your meaning, it ceases to care about your emotional truth or about the play's situation and theme. Diction, then, is crucial to the theatre at every level.

EXERCISE 19–1
REPEATED SENTENCES

Pair with a partner. Each partner selects a text, such as part of a play script or a narrative page from a book. The first partner begins by reading a sentence from the book. The second partner repeats it exactly, then reads a sentence from his or her book, which the first partner repeats.

Work up to longer and longer sentences. Concentrate on making your partner hear your text precisely and *understand* it. You have won the victory when your partner repeats the sentence perfectly and with complete comprehension.

Turn back-to-back and continue.

EXERCISE 19–2
SHAW SPEECH

Few playwrights rely on diction as much as George Bernard Shaw, whose plays contain brilliant verbal arguments about a multitude of still-pertinent issues. Memorize any short speech (about five sentences) from one of Shaw's plays and deliver it to your partner. Then ask your partner to paraphrase the content of the speech. Your "success" is not how well you spoke, but how well you "made" your partner hear and understand the speech.

Switch partners and repeat the speech, working harder to make precise points. Make your partner hear the speech for the first time.

Switch back to your original partner for a final time. Did you improve? Ask your partner.

Emphasis

Emphasis is the stuff of oral interpretation, the decision to make one word or syllable more important than another. Almost any line can be read with a variety of emphases. Look, for example, at Macbeth's line to his wife, after murdering Duncan: "I have done the deed."

I have done the deed. (It was *me!*)

I *have* done the deed. (You thought I wouldn't, didn't you?)

I have *done* the deed. (It's all over now.)

I have done *the* deed. (It's the most *important* deed I've ever done.)

I have done the *deed.* (It's just a "deed," nothing more.)

All of those emphases are justifiable, but you can play only one of them. Which one fits the interpretation, stimulates the action, and best serves your production of the play? Should there be subemphases, or equal emphases, such as "I have *done* the *deed*"? Emphasis, in a produced play, is often indicated by the director; more often, however, you will have to make these selections yourself.

Guiding your choice of emphasis should be the question, What do I want the other character(s) to hear and understand? Like diction, emphasis is a communication device; it should stimulate the right kinds of responses from the other person. What does Macbeth want his wife to understand from his utterance? If he worries that she is taking too much control, he may emphasize *I.* If he thinks she may want to turn back, he may emphasize *done.* If he thinks she may become hysterical, he may emphasize *deed.* Emphasis, then, is closely related to VOTE components, to the victory (intention) of your character, and the tactics you choose to implement that victory.

How do you emphasize a word? In the English language, increased stress and volume are the most common ways—that is, by saying the word a bit louder, and pronouncing the consonants a bit more precisely, "biting off" the word. But *coloring the vowels* of the word—giving them an enhanced, elongated, possibly unexpected *tone*—is often a more effective way of providing special emphasis. (In French, elongating and coloring vowels is the most common means of creating emphasis.) Creating emphasis through stress alone can result in strident, mechanical speaking (appropriate for certain characters, of course); adding to that emphasis by carefully shaded tonal variations can create a more evocative, "poetic" speech useful in establishing more subtle relationships.

EXERCISE 19–3
CHANGE OF EMPHASIS

With a partner, and by turns, deliver Macbeth's line "I have done the deed" with each of the five emphases described above, trying to capture the specific interpersonal meaning of each separate emphasis. Experiment with added stress and with coloring (elongating or enhancing) the vowels. How many of these emphases can you justify to yourself?

Select other lines that lend themselves to experimentation with different emphases, and see how many ways you can play them. Consider this exercise an experiment, however, and don't try to choose a "best" emphasis: That choice can come only from studying the play. Some possible lines, all from Shakespeare:

HAMLET: The time is out of joint. O cursed spite,

   That ever I was born to set it right!

KING LEAR: Dost thou call me fool, boy?

OTHELLO: I do not think but Desdemona's honest.

JULIET: You kiss by the book.

CLEOPATRA: O never was there Queen

   So mightily betrayed!

EXERCISE 19–4
PUNCTUATE WITH EMPHASIS

Using stress and tone emphasis alone, make the meaning of these sentences clear by speaking them to someone:

1. Replace "don't" with "won't."
2. That that is, is; that that is not, is not.
3. She would, would she?
4. Look at "Casanova" over there!
5. What do you mean, "Do my duty?" Duty demands dying!

Inflection

Inflection is, quite literally, the "turn" of the voice, usually by pitch, sometimes by tone and pitch. Often a rising pitch indicates a question. A sarcastic inflection, which substitutes a falling pitch for a rising one, unmistakably reverses the literal meaning of a line, making a giant difference in its content. For example: "That's great!" with a rising inflection, means what it says. But "That's great!" with a falling inflection, particularly when accompanied by a smirk or a raised eyebrow, means "That's terrible!" Needless to say, you must play these inflections with care.

If you listen to ordinary conversations, particularly involved conversations or arguments, you will hear a great variety in pitches and intonations, and rapid shifts in the pacing and forcefulness of the spoken words. Similarly, varied inflections and a wide range of pitches and volume levels characterize exciting stage dialog. The beginning actor, often handicapped by a sketchily memorized text and ample levels of stage fright, frequently speaks in a monotonous tone with steady pitch (poor Johnny One-Note) and falling inflections that dwindle away before the line comes to an end. Continually falling inflections—of the sort you hear when someone is reading off a laundry list—identify the technically untrained actor and make the play die a slow death. Monotone is as unlifelike as it is untheatrical, so you need not worry about learning it—unless your part consists of reading off a laundry list!

In general, rising reflections *sustain* the action of a speech, and falling inflections *conclude* (or try to conclude) it. A rising inflection demands an answer or a response; a falling inflection suggests an attempt to close off discussion or to have the last word. Thus:

$$\underline{\text{Shall we } go? \nearrow}$$

virtually demands an answer, and suggests that the person so invited can accept or refuse. Conversely,

$$\overline{\text{Shall we } go? \searrow}$$

while still technically an invitation, suggests that the "going" has already been decided; the person "asked" is merely requested to nod assent and leave. Falling inflections are characteristic of curtain lines:

The play is done.

and of argument-enders:

No more excuses!

Rising inflections are characteristic of real questions:

Are you going out?

or:

Are you going out?

and of questions that imply, "Don't you agree with me?"

I think she's sad. ["Don't you?"]

We shall have more to say later about inflections, particularly rising end-of-line inflections, which prove to be the principal key to linking dialog lines, sustaining long speeches, and building a scene to its climax. Here let it suffice to say that a variety of pitches and intonations, with *generally* rising inflections, are characteristic of both enthusiastic discussions and good technique in acting.

Rising inflections reflect growing interest, which excites fellow actors and audience alike. Falling inflections, particularly the trailed-off falling inflections beginners are overly prone to use (and which are characteristic of rote-memorized and rote-recited lines), lead to diminishing interest, growing boredom, and incipient stupor—in the actor and audience alike. Good inflections are varied, are taken from life, and are the echo of good conversation and involved argument. The technique of inflecting recaptures the rising inflections of lively speech, stimulates your acting partners (and the audience) with what you have to say, and compels your acting partners to interact vigorously with your character.

EXERCISE 19–5

I PLEDGE ALLEGIANCE

Recite the pledge of allegiance to the flag. Notice in yourself and others that the recited inflections are invariably (and monotonously) falling ones.

Now imagine that you are a turn-of-the-century immigrant landing on American shores after an escape from Old World oppression and an arduous journey. You arrive at a lovely green field where the American flag flies boldly. You approach the flag and create, on the spot, a prose poem of allegiance to the flag (that is, you improvise and say the pledge of allegiance on the spot). Take your time.

In Exercise 19–5, how did your inflections differ in your recitations of the pledge? How did other people's inflections differ in the same improvisation? How different did you feel when you *created* the pledge, instead of merely reciting it?

Every speech you say, as a character, should be delivered as *created*, not *recited*, by you. You, not the playwright, should be perceived as the originator of your lines. Inflections are a technical manifestation of the extent to which you create rather than recite your text.

Phrasing

Considered together, diction, emphasis, and inflection result in phrasing. Phrasing can never be separated from the VOTE principles that give your speeches meaning and give your character the lifeblood to mean them and speak them. But your character's ability to phrase speeches and to seek victory through words and rhetorical expression is something you, the actor, must supply.

As a first step, you should mark your script with underlines to indicate emphases. Add other notations pertaining to diction, based on the general principles of this lesson.

Which words should be elongated, to reach the other's character's consciousness? Which words should be stressed? Are there any sarcastic inflections? Argument-enders? Questions demanding answers? Statements begging for agreement? Ideas needing precise clarification? More generally, how does the character use language and rhetorical expression to further his or her cause? How does the character's vocabulary and syntax come into play in the character-to-character relationship? How does the character's phrasing show what kind of a thinker he or she is? What kind of tones does the character use? How much of a poet is he or she? How much of a bureaucrat? How does the character's VOTE translate into the character's phrasing?

Summary

Diction, emphasis, and inflection are ingredients of phrasing, which is the way the character uses words to influence events and other characters. Good phrasing has both a real-life similarity and theatrical effectiveness; it clarifies and focuses dialog, gives specific emphasis to the most important points of a scene or play, and sustains the excitement of the action and the enthusiasm of the characters. Varied and rising pitches are particularly useful as technical adjuncts to the VOTE-determined excitement of good acting.

Attack

The First Word

Attack is the delivery of the first word of a speech. The principal rule of attacking a speech is that you must come in strong—with confidence, vigor, and enthusiasm and also with substantial volume and pace. The weak attack, common in beginners, is filled with uncertainty, reflecting the beginner's characteristic uneasiness.

There are two reasons why your attack must be strong: a technical reason and a real-life reason. Technically, the actor must attack each speech vigorously in order to get the attention (focus) of the audience immediately at the outset of each speech. Remember, the audience does not know where to look from moment to moment, therefore it is up to you, the actor, to "pull" its attention every time you have something to say. The timid actor succeeds in doing this only by midsentence; the bold actor captures attention on the first syllable.

In real life a strong attack is even more important: In life, no playwright gives you the "right to speak." People don't automatically fall silent just because it's "your line." In life you must *earn* your opportunity to speak, and by the force of your speaking you must make everybody else stop talking and listen. This process is called *turn-taking* by conversation analysts, and it is as natural to life as it is (or should be) to the stage.

Thus the professional actor knows that he or she must "take stage" with both speeches and movement. You must not sink into the artificial comfort of the script with its preplanned alternation of "my lines and your lines." The professional actor *seizes* the floor powerfully with the first syllable of each speech. Thus attack defines your presence and earns you the right to speak as a character and to shape the scene you are in.

Sheer volume is normally a key ingredient of a strong attack. The uncertain actor, worried about making a mistake ("Is that my cue?" "Am I saying the right line?"), often reduces volume to minimize the magnitude of any possible error—committing a graver mistake in the process. In the theatre, it is almost always better to do something wrong boldly than to do something right timidly; so you should learn to give yourself the extra advantage of full projection on each opening syllable.

Volume alone is not the only attack device, however. Lengthening or coloring the vowel, sighing into an initial vowel, using an unusually high pitch, making a broad physical gesture or a noisy one, or overemphasizing an initial plosive consonant (the *p* in *perhaps*, perhaps) will also intensify your attack. So will opening your eyes wider, taking in a big gulp of air, rising from your chair, bouncing up on your toes, or taking a step forward.

Remember, all of these "technical" actions are taken from ordinary life. Observe two people in an involved conversation or an argument and you will see most if not all of these turn-taking techniques coming into play—quite unconsciously and, more important, quite unselfconsciously. See if you can put each of these attack devices into a patch of dialog you and your partner have already memorized.

The *pace* of your attack is a second major consideration. Normally your attack should be fast rather than slow, despite the beginner's tendency to be slow rather than fast.

Why should your attack be fast? Technically, to speed up the action of the play. In the final rehearsals, most directors admonish the actors to "pick up your cues!" Elapsed time between lines—the pauses of slow attacks—are wasted time as far as the audience is concerned; they are getting no information and they have no idea what you are thinking about during your "pregnant pause." Indeed, they don't even know where to look, since they have no idea whose line is coming next.

In real life, people do not simply trade lines in alternation; they *break* into conversations and *interrupt* each other. They are *eager* to speak rather than simply obliged to say lines. To re-create that sort of high-intensity conversation, directors ask actors to pick up their cues, to portray a vivid discussion rather than a listless one.

When you attack a speech with pace, you are responding much more directly to your partner's line. Your emotions, stimulated by your partner, will be in full flush only for a split second: If you respond at that moment, your response will be filled with feeling; if you wait a second or two, that feeling will be dissipated. In acting, your most intense feelings should occur *while you're speaking*, not before or after, and you must seize the moment when you are most moved, not the moment a half-second later, to attack your speech.

Taking Turns

A strong attack does not mean that you cannot pause during your speech, of course, or that you must race through your lines. Far from it. A strong attack means that you cannot pause unnecessarily *before* your speech, but that you seize the stage first—and then develop your nuances afterward. A good playwright will help you by giving you strong "turn-taking" attack words at the beginning of your speeches.

EXERCISE 20–1

TURN-TAKING DIALOG

Read to yourself, and then aloud with a partner, this scene between two teenagers. The "she" in the first line refers to Eva's mother. Read the scene aloud several times with attention to making strong attacks.

ROBERT: Where does she think we go?

EVA: Oh, I tell her we just go walking in the woods, talking. She knows that but she thinks we do other things too.

ROBERT: Like what?

EVA: You know.

ROBERT: Like what?

EVA: You know. Dirty things.

ROBERTS: What does she think that for?

EVA: I don't tell her, though.

ROBERT: What would you tell her?

EVA: About that. About when I have to pee and things.

ROBERT: Well, there's nothing dirty about that.

EVA: Well, don't you think I know!

ROBERT: She means other things.

EVA: What?

ROBERT: Never mind.

EVA: Well, don't you think I know?

(Lanford Wilson, The Rimers of Eldritch)

The scene in Exercise 20–1, fraught with repressed sexual curiosity and suspense (it will lead to a clumsy attempted rape and a shooting), is filled with awkwardness and hesitancy. The dialog clearly is not meant for racing through. Nonetheless, the scene develops its anxious intensity only if the attacks are continuously strong. Notice how Wilson, the playwright, has placed attack words such as *oh* and *well*, which can be attacked on cue and then followed by a pause. Each character speaks quickly in order to seize the conversation from the other—and then pauses to figure out what to say. Notice also how Eva uses "You know" as a temporizing answer: to make Robert stop asking embarrassing questions, and yet to answer in a noncommittal way.

Thus all characters in dialog try to control the conversation—even when they wish to cease conversing or cease answering questions—but the only way to do that is with a strong attack, not a weak one.

Study this dialog, which is a more forceful argument. This is the scene in which Hamlet stabs Polonius, who is hiding behind a curtain.

HAMLET: Now, mother, what's the matter?

QUEEN: Hamlet, thou hast thy father much offended.

HAMLET: Mother, you have my father much offended.

QUEEN: Come, come, you answer with an idle tongue.

HAMLET: Go, go, you question with a wicked tongue.

QUEEN: Why, how now, Hamlet!

HAMLET: What's the matter now?

QUEEN: Have you forgot me?

HAMLET: No, by the rood, not so;
You are the queen, your husband's brother's wife.
And—would it were not so—you are my mother.

QUEEN: Nay, then, I'll set those to you that can speak.

HAMLET: Come, come, and sit you down; you shall not budge;
You go not till I set you up a glass
Where you may see the inmost part of you.

QUEEN: What wilt thou do? Thou wilt not murder me?
Help, help, ho!

POLONIUS [*Behind a curtain*]: What, ho! help, help, help!

HAMLET [*Drawing his sword*]: How now! A rat? [*Stabbing through the curtain*] Dead, for a ducat, dead!

POLONIUS [*Behind*]: O, I am slain!

QUEEN: O me, what hast thou done?

HAMLET: Nay, I know not: Is it the king?

QUEEN: O, WHAT A RASH AND BLOODY DEED IS THIS!

HAMLET: A bloody deed! Almost as bad, good mother,
As kill a king, and marry with his brother.

QUEEN: As kill a king!

HAMLET: Ay, lady, 'twas my word.

(William Shakespeare, *Hamlet*)

Shakespeare's dialog, in general, displays masterful turn-taking. Shakespeare was an actor as well as a playwright, and consequently his verse is the most "actable" in the English language. The vast majority of Shakespearean speeches—perhaps 90 percent or more—begin with one-syllable words, which are the easiest to attack, particularly in a verse form (iambic pentameter) that stresses the second, not the first, syllable. And in Shakespeare, polysyllabic opening words are usually commands, interjections, the names of the characters addressed, or repeated words from the previous line, all of which are easy to attack strongly.

In the scene from *Hamlet,* all possible turn-taking devices are in play: repeated attention-getters ("Come, come"), characters' names ("Hamlet," "Mother"), interjections ("O"), temporizers ("Why," "How now!") and monosyllables, often in combination. Read that scene with a partner, finding how you can make strong attacks and still leave some room for pauses within several of the lines.

Preparing Strong Attacks

Understanding the dramatic need for the strong attack, how do you go about creating it onstage?

Confidence in your lines, and in your character's tactics and intentions, is paramount. Weak attacks almost never come from conscious decision, but rather derive from actor trepidation. (Remember when you were in your elementary school choir and were shy about singing your first notes until you could confirm that everyone else was singing with you?)

Preparation, however, is a specific key to delivering strong attacks. Remember that the line cue is the actual word you come in after; the action cue is the word or phrase in the previous speech that prompts you to prepare your own speech. Thus:

QUEEN: Have you forgot me?
HAMLET: No, . . .

Me is the line cue; *forgot* is the action cue. When the Queen has said, "Have you forgot . . . ," Hamlet already knows what she's asking and is preparing his reply before she has finished her sentence. Thus when she completes her question, the word *no* is already on the tip of his tongue, ready to fly out.

Go through your script and underline all the action cues in your partner's lines—the words that tell you what you need to know before you really *want* to speak up. If you become aware of action cues, you will be able to understand—and portray—your *character* by picking up your partner's cues and delivering your lines with a strong attack, rather than merely following a technical command of the director.

EXERCISE 20–2

ACTION CUES

Pair with a partner and select a short, intense, two-person scene made up of very short speeches. Underline all the action cues. Analyze all the turn-taking devices. Then read the scene aloud, emphasizing the attack points as much as possible without racing the lines.
   Memorize, rehearse, and play the scene as you have studied it.

Summary

Attack, which is the delivery of the first word of your line, is a crucial technical element of the stage because it focuses attention on the speaking person and conveys the idea that your character *wants* to speak—and not that you are speaking only because the playwright has ordered you to. In the theatre, as in life, you must earn your right to speak; you must take the stage by the forcefulness of your speaking, and your vocal attack is the principal way by which you do this. Strong attack requires substantial volume, energy, clarity, and pace. You can prepare for strong attacks by studying your cue lines for action cues that spur your response shortly before it actually comes, so that you will be fully ready to speak on your line cue. Picking up cues, via the strong attack, does not mean rushing or racing your lines. Pauses taken after a strong attack—within the body of your line rather than before your line—can be even more effective if the attacks in the scene are uniformly strong ones.

Follow-Through

The "Hook"

As it is important to "pick up your cues," so it is important not to "drop the end of your sentences." The last word of each speech must be audible and intelligible. So directors have urged beginning actors since time immemorial.

Beginning actors often drop the ends of their sentences or their speeches. When they come to the end of their scripted words, they sort of glide to a stop in the manner of a newly licensed driver gently pulling into a parking place.

But intentions continue beyond the end of the line. The end of the speech is the moment when you are trying to compel your partner—the other character in your scene—to agree with you, or yield to you, or do your bidding in one fashion or another.

In acting, every line you speak must stimulate a reaction or a response from the other characters. Metaphorically, your line must "hook" the attention of your acting partner and demand that your partner react in some way or other. A weak follow-through has no hook—and consequently will catch no fish, no matter how beautifully cast.

Questions as Questions

The easiest lines to follow through are questions—simply because a question forces your partner to respond. When you ask,

"Where are you going?" the question mark (which resembles a hook!) demands an answer and by so doing pulls your partner *and the audience* into your situation. When asked with real inter-rogative compulsion, questions create immediate drama; for that reason, they are used as the opening lines in a great number of dramatic masterpieces:

"When shall we three meet again?"—*Macbeth*

"What is it, children?"—*Oedipus*

"What's the matter?"—*Major Barbara*

"Now what's got into you?"—*The Misanthrope*

"Who's there?"—*Hamlet*

Because of their immediacy and their focus on the other person (the askee), questions can be played forcefully and followed through with rising—not falling—excitement.

And yet beginning actors tend to play questions as state-ments, and with falling inflections rather than the rising inflec-tion that is both more dramatic and more true to real-life questioning. For example, many beginning actors will tend to ask

"Where are you going?"

rather than:

"Where are you going?"

or:

"Where are you going?"

or:

"Where are you go ing?"

Perhaps the falling inflection sounds sophisticated (at least it certainly sounds "superior"). More likely, carelessness results from knowing that the other actor is forced to respond anyway, because the script says so. But the falling inflection is both un-lifelike and uninvolving—a flat statement rather than a demand for information. Try asking the question to a partner both ways, and notice how your partner responds to the various inflections.

The first rule of following through is to ask real questions. Give rising end-inflections as you look your partner—the askee —in the eye: *Demand an answer* with your inflection and your expression. *Care* what that answer is. If you do this, everyone will hear the ends of your sentences, and you will create intense interaction on stage as you yield the floor—for the moment—to your acting partner.

Statements as Questions

While it is unwise, most of the time, to turn your questions into statements, it is usually quite desirable to turn your statements into questions. Most statements are, in fact, invocations if not direct questions: Most statements "ask" the other person to agree, or to praise the speaker, or to accept the speaker's wishes, plans, or definitions. "I'm going out" is a statement responding to the previous question, but it also can be inflected to ask a variety of implicit questions:

I'm going out. (Do you want to come?)
I'm going out. (Would you rather I'd stay?)
I'm going out. (Are you going to ask me where?)
I'm going out. (Do you want to make plans for my return?)

Again, the upward inflection of the last word, the gaze and expression of the actor speaking, and the intentions played between actors can make the line an effective stage communication, not just a flat statement of fact. Follow-through is crucial here. The line must *lead* somewhere, must demand a reaction or a response. If you can find the hidden question in the otherwise declarative speech, you can hook the other actor—and through him or her, the audience—with the parting word or syllable.

EXERCISE 21–1

MAKING QUESTIONS

Play the following lines to "hook" your partner by ending them with an upward inflection. Make each line into either a question or an implicit question (a request for a favorable response or confirmation). Put pressure on your partner: Play for the victory of your partner's favorable response.

1. Are you sure you won't have some oatmeal?
2. How long have I been back? Six months? Seven?
3. May one still speak of time?
4. It's time for me to go!
5. What are you thinking of?
6. How comest thou hither, tell me, and wherefore?
7. I hope you're not going to make a nuisance of yourself.
8. I said, go answer the door. What are you, deaf?
9. Seems to me you were staring through the window at me.
10. I believe my attitude must be deemed the proper one.

These are all lines from well-known plays. Number four is Vershinin's attempted leave-taking from Olga at the end of Chekhov's *The Three Sisters*. As he is waiting for Masha to arrive, he doesn't leave. His line is a request for Olga to say, "Wait, don't go."

Find reasons to make all these lines similar requests.

Statements as Statements

Some statements are intended to close a discussion or end a relationship. "I am going out!" spoken very firmly, with a downward inflection on the last syllable and perhaps a gesture of finality (pointing to the floor, shaking the fist), conveys the message that "as far as I am concerned, there is no more to be said on this subject!" The most powerful lines, said in this fashion, can literally leave the other character speechless:

LADY BRITOMART: Charles Lomax: if you can behave yourself, behave yourself. If not, leave the room. (*Lomax . . . sits on the settee . . . quite overcome.*)

(George Bernard Shaw, *Major Barbara*)

TOM: You'll go up, up on a broomstick, over Blue Mountain with seventeen gentlemen callers! You ugly—babbling old—*witch!* (*Amanda is . . . stunned and stupefied . . .*)

(Tennesee Williams, *The Glass Menagerie*)

LINDA: You're a pair of animals! Not one, not another living soul would have had the cruelty to walk out on that man in a restaurant!

BIFF: (*Not looking at her*) Is that what he said?

LINDA: He didn't have to say anything. He was so humiliated he nearly limped when he came in.

HAPPY: But, Mom, he had a great time with us . . .

LINDA: (*Cutting him off violently*) Shut up! (*Without another word, Happy goes upstairs.*)

(Arthur Miller, *Death of a Salesman*)

These strong declarations provoke momentary speechlessness, as the original stage directions make clear. But you can use many such lines to attempt to "win going away." One of the differences between a scripted argument and a real one is that, in life, you are not trying to sustain dialog; you are trying to end the argument, with yourself as the victor, each time you speak. You are always trying to create "the last word." Strong follow-through attempts to create that lifelike situation; in an argument, the last word of your speech is played as what you hope will be the last word on the subject. Notice that Linda's "Shut up!" in the *Death of a Salesman* quotation has both a strong attack and a strong follow-through, as mandated by the author's stage directions. It is a particularly powerful climactic moment of theatre for that reason.

Invocations to "Shut up"—that is, speeches intended to leave the others speechless—generally conclude with a highly stressed and downwardly inflected terminal syllable. They need not be shouted (notice Lady Britomart's elegant tone). And they need not be successful. (Tom's denunciation of his mother actually fails, as he exits the room clumsily, breaking his sister's glass menagerie as he goes.) Nevertheless, these lines should be played as your character's attempt to achieve a victory: to make the disagreeing characters be quiet, recognize your character's correctness (or authority), and yield to your character's point of view or leadership. The "hook" of the last word should be intense, accompanied by continued eye contact (are they obeying?) and physical assurance.

EXERCISE 21–2
ARGUMENT-ENDERS

Give the following speeches to a partner, foreclosing all discussion. Use downward inflections to close each speech. Try to make any reply virtually impossible.

1. Get out!
2. The matter is closed!
3. I'll see you in court.
4. We shall never surrender.
5. Honor thy father and thy mother.
6. I may vomit.

Trail-offs

Not all speeches have a "hook" at the end. Some speeches just trail off. Tennessee Williams wrote a play (*In the Bar of a Tokyo Hotel*) in which more than three-quarters of the speeches end in midsentence. Sometimes characters realize they've said all they really mean before they've completed their sentence. Sometimes they forget what they were saying while speaking; sometimes they just lapse into dreamland. Sometimes characters trail off in their speeches simply because they understand only too well that they needn't complete their words in order to communicate their thoughts.

Playing trail-offs is dangerous for the beginner because the communication must be sustained on deeper and subtler levels, without the support of the follow-through "hook." But the actor should be prepared for the occasional speech that winds into one's own reflections rather than hooking into the partner for a response.

Summary

Effective follow-through on the last words of your speech is a "hook" demanding a reaction from the other character. Questions hook your partner when they are asked with a rising inflection and direct eye contact. Statements can be used like questions to provoke a response. Statements calculated to provoke silence from the partner can be used as attempts to end arguments and force agreement. Expression, gaze, and inflection (generally upward for questions, downward for statements) are the ingredients of the successful "hook."

Line Linkage

Analyzing Dialog

Attack and follow-through are not just isolated parts of your speeches; they are integrated elements of free-flowing dialog. The link between lines of dialog—between your partner's follow-through and your attack and vice versa—is a primary technical key to building a scene's intensity.

Study the following dialog between Tom and his mother in *The Glass Menagerie*:

AMANDA: What are you looking at?

TOM: The moon.

AMANDA: Is there a moon this evening?

TOM: It's rising over Garfinkel's Delicatessen.

AMANDA: So it is! A little silver slipper of a moon. Have you made a wish on it yet?

TOM: Um-hum.

AMANDA: What did you wish for?

TOM: That's a secret.

AMANDA: A secret, huh? Well, I won't tell mine either. I will be just as mysterious as you.

TOM: I bet I can guess what yours is.

AMANDA: Is my head so transparent?

TOM: You're not a sphinx.

AMANDA: No, I don't have secrets. I'll tell you what I wished for on the moon. Success and happiness for my precious children! I wish for that whenever there's a moon, and when there isn't a moon, I wish for it, too.

TOM: I thought perhaps you wished for a gentleman caller.

AMANDA: Why do you say that?

TOM: Don't you remember asking me to fetch one?

AMANDA: I remember suggesting that it would be nice for your sister if you brought home some nice young man from the warehouse. I think that I've made that suggestion more than once.

TOM: Yes, you have made it repeatedly.

AMANDA: Well?

TOM: We are going to have one.

AMANDA: *What?*

TOM: A gentleman caller!

AMANDA: You mean you have asked some nice young man to come over?

TOM: Yep. I've asked him to dinner.

AMANDA: You really did?

TOM: I did!

AMANDA: You did, and did he—*accept?*

TOM: He did!

AMANDA: Well, well—well, well! That's—lovely!

TOM: I thought that you would be pleased.

AMANDA: It's definite, then?

TOM: Very definite.

AMANDA: Soon?

TOM: Very soon.

AMANDA: For heaven's sake, stop putting me on and tell me some things, will you?

TOM: What things do you want me to tell you?

AMANDA: *Naturally* I would like to know when he's *coming!*

TOM: He's coming tomorrow.

AMANDA: *Tomorrow?*

TOM: Yep. Tomorrow.

AMANDA: But, Tom!

TOM: Yes, Mother?

AMANDA: Tomorrow gives me no time!

TOM: Time for what?

AMANDA: Preparations!

(Tennessee Williams, The Glass Menagerie)

What actually transpires here? Very little, if you are looking only for plot, or for strictly narrative information. You could write the events of this scene in one or two sentences. But Williams has written forty-six speeches. Why? To build a relationship, of course. What transpires is an exchange of feelings between a son and a mother; it is a carefully arranged interchange of strokings, put-downs, requests for attention, attempts to charm, attempts to out wit, attempts to achieve dominance, attempts to surprise. These speeches demonstrate the artistry of superbly crafted *dramatic* dialog, as contrasted to narrative storytelling: The relationships are expressed through verbal interaction, not by description.

You can analyze this interchange of dialog for line-linkage characteristics. First, study the particular attack and follow-through techniques. Notice that the writing is peppered with questions (eighteen of them), even questions that answer questions: ". . . tell me some things, will you?" "What things do you want me to tell you?" Words repeated from line to line develop the impact of a musical refrain: "You really did?" "I did!" "You did, and did he—*accept?*" "He did!" Notice how Williams stresses attack and follow-through words in "*Naturally* I would like to know when he's *coming!*" Finally, notice how Williams uses pauses within the dialog, without interfering with the attacks or follow-throughs:

AMANDA: . . . and did he—*accept?*

TOM: He did!

AMANDA: Well, well—well, well! That's—lovely!

The three pauses, marked by dashes in the original, give Amanda a time to reflect, to relish her victory, and to formulate her considered opinion of Tom's act, without slowing the attacks or trailing off the follow-throughs.

Rising End-Inflections

The key to linkage is that the follow-through of one speech sets up the attack of the next speech, much like a springboard sets up a dive. Attacking from a weak cue is like diving from a broken springboard.

Look at the first four lines of Williams' dialog: two questions and two answers. If the questions are posed and inflected as questions, the following speeches will be dramatically easy to attack. If they are simply stated with falling inflections, however, the following lines will be off to a deadly start. Witness:

AMANDA: What are you looking at?

TOM: The moon.

AMANDA: Is there a moon this evening?

TOM: It's rising over Garfinkel's Delicatessen.

This is "laundry list" acting. The speeches are simply read off as lines on a list; the inflections create no pressure on Tom, no interaction between the actors at the emotional level, and no compulsion for the audience to care. Compare with:

AMANDA: What are you looking at?

TOM: The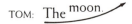

AMANDA:

TOM: It's <u>rising over Garfinkel's Delicat</u>essen.

No attempt should be made to specify the "best" inflection of these speeches. Both ways of playing those lines are "valid," in the sense that people can and do talk that way some of the time. The second way, however, is brighter, more energetic, more interactive, and builds more momentum. The rising inflections give a lift to the interchange and a life to the feelings that pass between the actors.

In general, rising end-inflections are the technical key to keeping a scene alive, and to developing the momentum of line linkage. They are crucial in *building* a scene, because they lead somewhere. Rising inflections are lifelike as well as dramatic: In real life, if you are asking questions, arguing points, responding playfully, teasing, challenging, demanding, amusing, or persuading, you are probably using a preponderance of rising inflections in your speech. Conversely, if you are dutifully rote-reciting, you are probably using mostly falling (and weakly falling) inflections. Actors have a term for weak, downwardly inflected cues: "He handed me a dead fish." Better to give your fellow actor a springboard: It is more lifelike, more stimulating, and more dramatic all at the same time.

Falling End-Inflections

Falling end-inflections can be used to create transitions: to end an argument, to change the subject or the mood, all without creating an unneeded pause.

AMANDA: So‿on?

TOM: Very so‿on.

AMANDA: For heaven's sake, stop . . .

Tom's falling end-inflection on *soon* makes clear to Amanda that she'll get no further with him on that line of questioning, so she has to try another tack. Her "for heaven's sake" is a temporizing phrase, one that she can attack strongly and right on cue—but one that's noncommital enough to suggest she doesn't know exactly what she's going to say next. Noncommital phrases, such as interjections, give the character (and the actor) thinking time; they permit a rapid superficial attack while you are simultaneously summoning up your reserves for the stronger attack that immediately follows.

Attack Inflections

Attack inflections, or "front inflections," are the dive you make off the end-inflection springboard. The most exciting attack inflections come in at a *higher pitch* than the preceding end-inflection. Study this linkage:

AMANDA: What did you wish for? TOM: That's a secret.

Compare with this reading, common among beginning actors:

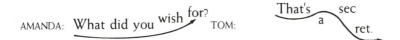

AMANDA: What did you wish for? TOM: That's a secret.

An answer that "comes in on top of" (at a higher pitch than) an upward-inflected question shows a character seizing control of a scene, rather than dutifully responding to an investigation. Attacks that come in low (in pitch, not in energy) can show something else. For example:

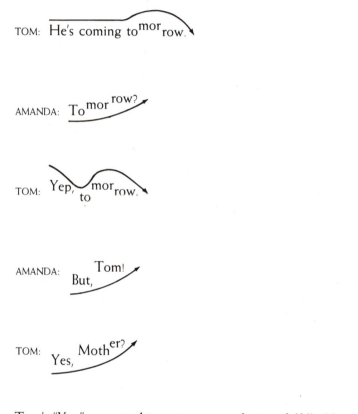

TOM: He's coming to^{mor}row.

AMANDA: To^{mor} ^{row?}

TOM: Yep, to mor row.

AMANDA: But, Tom!

TOM: Yes, Moth^{er?}

Tom's "Yep" suggests his excitement at having fulfilled her command, forcing her to deal with the immediacy of his action, forcing her to deal with him on his own terms. (Williams' use of the slang *yep* also suggests this.) Tom's "Yes," however, in response to her implied criticism ("But, Tom!") might begin on a low-pitched attack, perhaps in conscious self-mockery of his subservience.

Sometimes the lines call for a playful attack in your follow-through. For example:

AMANDA: Tomorrow gives me no time!

TOM: Time for what?

Tom's repetition of Amanda's follow-through words in his attack gives him an opportunity to repronounce her word, perhaps mocking her inflection (or accent, or note of hysteria) as he rephrases the issue. Note, of course, that Tom knows exactly what Amanda means by "no time." His line is only a rhetorical ploy—thus emphasizing the relationship between technical aspects of line linkage and real-life aspects of person-to-person (including child-to-parent) interaction.

Pauses

Pauses play an important role in dialog. In the plays of Samuel Beckett and Harold Pinter, for example, pauses have become famous. Look at the following scene from Pinter's *Betrayal*:

ROBERT: Speak.

JERRY: Yes.

(Pause)

ROBERT: You look quite rough.

(Pause)

    What's the trouble?

(Pause)

    It's not about you and Emma, is it?

(Pause)

    I know all about that.

JERRY: Yes. So I've . . . been told.

ROBERT: Ah.

(Pause)

    Well, it's not very important, is it?

Five stipulated pauses, plus one ellipsis (. . .) indicating a sixth, in a scene of less than three dozen words, clearly demonstrate unusual line linkage. The pauses, however, can be integrated in the scene because of the intense interest each character has in the other's thoughts. The action continues through the silences with the intensity of each character's investigation of the other. Robert still must ask his questions so as to demand answers—that is, with rising inflections—and then Jerry's silences will be answer enough. The pauses that follow are virtually deafening. Even Robert's "Ah" is an invocation for Jerry to speak, and when he doesn't, we know Jerry's extreme discomfort by what he *doesn't* do.

Pauses serve as line linkage when they are not mere lapses, or when they are not just a comfortable rest stop that the actor needs to collect his or her thoughts and feelings. Awkward pauses, even momentary ones, become holes in the dialog, where the actor's energy falls out of the scene and where the audience's attention begins to wander. In order to be effective, both for actor and for audience, the pause must be part of the linkage between lines: It must betoken *something that does not happen* instead of *just nothing happening.*

Long Speeches

A long speech in a play also requires good line linkage, but here the linkage is between your first clause or sentence and your second, and so on until the end. A long speech is not simply a series of sentences; it is an integrated expression. If it is to have a lifelike vitality, the components of that expression must develop an integrated momentum.

Rising inflections are generally the means of sustaining a long speech. A rising inflection means that you have something more to say, that you haven't yet completed your thoughts. Falling inflections are idea-enders; they suggest you have come to the end of your thoughts. If you haven't come to the end, then you must start your speech all over again, which causes a break in the audience's attention.

Look at the following speech from Shaw's *Man and Superman*:

RAMSDEN: I will not allow you or any man to treat me as if I were a mere member of the British public. I detest its prejudices; I scorn its narrowness: I demand the right to think for myself. You pose as an advanced man. Let me tell you that I was an advanced man before you were born.

Beginning actors tend to use a falling inflection before every period and every semicolon. This tendency deadens the dialog and requires the beginner's partner to overcome the inertia of fallen inflections after each clause (something like running a 100-yard dash and stopping every ten feet). Try reading the speech aloud with rising inflections on *public, prejudices, narrowness, myself,* and *man;* then with a dramatically falling inflection on the terminal *born.* The speech is much easier to sustain if you can learn to speak it this way.

Coming In "On Top"

Coming in at a higher pitch than your cue—particularly when your cue is upwardly inflected—creates exceptional momentum and excitement. Consider these examples:

A: Where are you go$^{ing?}$ B: Out!

A: What are you do$^{ing?}$ B: Noth$_{ing!}$

Notice how the attack of the answer springs off the "hook" of the question, as the actor seizes the stage with authority. The actor who can "come in on top" of his or her cues is well suited to playing a character staying "on top" of his or her situation, and the dialog between two or more such characters will be dramatically thrilling.

EXERCISE 22–1

LINE LINKING

Select a six- or seven-line sequence from the Tom-Amanda scene. With a partner, analyze the sequence for line-linkage possibilities. Read through the lines, concentrating on finding the best possible linkings. Don't be afraid to devote your thinking to pure technical analysis. But as you grow comfortable repeating the sequence, try to understand how the inflections relate to the victories sought by your character, and the tactics used. Make the inflections "real" by trying to be yourself. Are these inflections *yours?* They should become yours.

EXERCISE 22–2

THE LONG SPEECH

Select any long speech from any prose play, preferably a speech that contains a sustained argument or explanation. In your study, try to find clauses or sentences that call for a rising end-inflection. Mark these in the text of the speech. Memorize and practice the speech until you feel comfortable with it. Deliver it. Are you able to sustain the argument or explanation?

Line Linking in Practice

Line linking, like any acting technique, should be learned in the classroom or studio to the point that it becomes an integral part of your acting instrument. During an acting performance, you should not be thinking about attacks, or follow-throughs, or inflections: You should be thinking solely about your victory and your VOTE. By that time, the technique of linking your lines to others should be unconscious and automatic. The better you understand the relationship between line linking on stage and line linking in daily life, the easier this technique will be.

Line linkage is rarely addressed in American acting schools, although it is considered a rudiment of actor training in Great Britain. It has obvious dangers: Nothing will make your acting seem more artificial than concentrating on line linking to the exclusion of all other techniques. Expert line linking is the result of the stage intuition and sense of timing that come from experience. The technique is extremely important in the finest acting you will *see,* and it should become part of the finest acting you will *do* as well.

Summary

Line linkage is not easily mastered, but some general principles can be understood and put into practice by the beginner: (1) Pauses are generally ineffective line links unless they indicate specific questions not answered, or roads not taken. (2) Rising end-inflections provide a springboard for your partner's next line and stimulate energetic dialog exchanges. Rising inflections sustain long speeches by acting as springboards for subequent sentences. (3) Strong attacks that come in at a higher pitch ("on top" of a cue—particularly a cue that is itself upwardly inflected) are extremely powerful dramatically. (4) Line linkages that are theatrically effective ordinarily reflect the liveliness of real-life conversation or argument; they are rhetorical features of dialog if the play's *characters* use rhetorical devices themselves.

Scene Structure

Dramatic Divisions

Plays are customarily divided into acts and scenes. These are ordinarily separated by intermissions (acts) or pauses in the action (scenes), and they are usually noted and numbered in the play script itself.

Not noted in the play script are two smaller divisions: *French scenes*, which begin and end with the entrance or exit of each named character, and *subscenes*, which are exchanges of dialog and action that center on a single basic event or line of argument. Subscenes are particularly important for the actor, for they are the basic units of acting scenes.

Within the subscene—which may be two lines or ten pages in length—are *beats* and *moments*. Beats are single units of action, corresponding to the beats in a musical measure. A role is made up of thousands of beats, just as a symphony is. Moments are usually construed as silent beats: moments of reflection when the character sizes up a situation before proceeding.

These terms are not precisely defined; the term *beat*, particularly, has been used in a wide variety of applications since Stanislavski introduced it early in the century. But such distinctions are useful in helping the actor divide any segment of dramatic material into separate units of varying meaning, intensity, and emotional charge.

Structural Characteristics

The basic structure of dramatic action is usually described as an inverted V listing to starboard (to the right). A conflict begins with some sort of incitement, escalates slowly to a peak of intensity, and breaks suddenly into some sort of release. The peak of the *intensity*—the top of the inverted V—is called the *climax;* the incitement is called the *inciting action;* and the release is called the *resolution* or *denouement.* The inverted V leans to starboard—that is, the build-up to the climax is slower than the collapse to resolution—because building to climax sustains audience interest almost indefinitely, whereas climax and resolution provide an aesthetic and emotional jolt that is immensely satisfying but essentially short-lived.

The basic structure is characteristic of plays and scenes and of subscenes as well: It is absolutely fundamental to the drama. Thus a play leads up to a climax, but so does every scene and subscene, albeit in a more restrained fashion. You can graph the action of a play thus:

Climax

Inciting action   Resolution

But if you look more closely at the lines in that graph, they are more accurately drawn as:

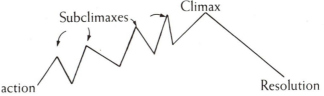

Subclimaxes   Climax

Inciting action   Resolution

The climax of a play, or of a scene, is of primary importance to the actor: It is not only the moment of maximum dramatic tension, it is also the moment when the issues of the play are most clearly defined and the emotions of the characters are most nakedly exposed. In classical dramaturgy (the study of dramatic form), the climax may bring about recognition (of higher truth or truths), reversal (of fortunes or thinking), and a catharsis (a profusion of feelings leading finally to their purification or "cleansing"). Climaxes in tragedies have been awesome: Oedipus gouging out his eyes, Hamlet slaying his uncle, and Phaedra taking a fatal poison. Climaxes of comedies are more subtle, but they are inevitably present in well-written and well-produced plays.

You must understand that dramatic structure is not merely a creation of the theatre, nor is it an artifice of dramatic writing. It is fundamental to life itself. It can be seen in explicit acts, such as sexual orgasm; in ritual enactments, such as the bullfight; in other aesthetic forms, such as the symphony; and in many public events, such as boxing matches, horse races, and auctions. In the long range the pattern can be seen in the cycle of life, in Shakespeare's "seven ages of man," and T. S. Eliot's "birth and copulation and death." That the pattern of life-rhythms can be represented by the aesthetic pattern of drama is one of the reasons why the theatre has been such a satisfying art for more than twenty-five hundred years.

Transitions

Transitions are the imaginary lines between scenes, between subscenes, and between the beats of an actor's performance. Transitions are changes: of attitudes, of actions, of understandings. Nothing communicates information about your character so effectively as your transitions, because change is inherently noticeable and meaningful. Frowning conveys concern, for example, but not so vividly, nor so precisely, as a smile that suddenly turns into a frown. That process of turning into, or turning, signals what a character is thinking. Frowning, by itself, is merely the exhibition of an attitude: a smile turning into a frown is an action that can be construed as motivated, intended (if not intentional), and meaningful.

Sharp transitions, as a rule, are more dramatically effective than muddy ones, partly because of the theatre's demand for compression and clarity, and partly because of the desirability of dramatic variety. The closer you can define the moment in a scene when love turns to hate, or the desire to conquer turns to the desire to escape, the more precisely and vividly you can play the actions on either side of the transition, and the more exciting you can make the transition itself. Thus defining transitions closely, and playing them sharply and boldly, is an important aspect of acting technique.

Scene Breakdown

We can study the elements of scene structure by looking at another passage from Williams' *The Glass Menagerie*: the French scene in Scene 3 between Tom and Amanda in which Tom argues with his mother about his lack of independence.

TOM: What in Christ's name am I—

AMANDA: *(Shrilly)* Don't you use that—

TOM: Supposed to do!

AMANDA: Expression! Not in my—

TOM: Ohhh!

AMANDA: Presence! Have you gone out of your senses?

TOM: I have, that's true, *driven* out!

AMANDA: What is the matter with you, you—big—big—IDIOT!

TOM: Look!—I've got *no thing*, no single thing—

AMANDA: Lower your voice!

TOM: In my life here that I can call my OWN! Everything is—

AMANDA: Stop that shouting!

TOM: Yesterday you confiscated my books! You had the nerve to—

AMANDA: I took that horrible novel back to the library—yes! That hideous book by that insane Mr. Lawrence. *(Tom laughs wildly.)* I cannot control the output of diseased minds or people who cater to them— *(Tom laughs still more wildly)* BUT I WON'T ALLOW SUCH FILTH BROUGHT INTO MY HOUSE! No, no, no, no, no!

TOM: House, house! Who pays rent on it, who makes a slave of himself to—

AMANDA: *(Fairly screeching)* Don't you DARE to—

TOM: No, no, I mustn't say things! *I've* got to just—

AMANDA: Let me tell you—

TOM: I don't want to hear any more! *(He tears the portieres open [and goes out, Amanda following].)*

AMANDA: You *will* hear more, you—

TOM: No, I won't hear more, I'm going out!

AMANDA: You come right back in—

TOM: Out, out, out! Because I'm—

AMANDA: Come back here, Tom Wingfield! I'm not through talking to you!

TOM: Oh, go—

LAURA: *(Desperately)* Tom!

AMANDA: You're going to listen, and no more insolence from you . . .

The French scene is here divided into four subscenes, each marked by added space above and below. (Except for this added space and one edited stage description, all punctuation and typographical emphasis is from the original text.) As a French scene, it begins with the two characters arguing and ends with Laura's intervention; the four subscenes define individual components of the mother-son quarrel. Each subscene begins with a topic word or phrase defining the component: "Christ's name," "no thing [that is mine]," "house," and "you *will* hear more." These topic words are the inciting actions of each subscene, each of which rises to a separate climax.

Williams has carefully provided each actor with climactic expressions, sometimes with intentionally incorrect grammar, sometimes with capitalized insults, sometimes with a rapid stage cross, and finally with Tom about to swear at his mother, and Laura—a new character to the scene—desperately entering the conflict and raising the level of tension by one full psyche. Each of these climaxes tops the previous one; this is the way arguments—and scenes—are built.

Notice also how Williams, one of the most skilled writers of American stage dialog, builds the rising intensity within the subscenes. Tom first laughs "wildly" and then "still more wildly," thus increasing the level of tension during his mother's speech. Repetitions are used to escalate effect, rather than to convey added content. Sometimes the escalation is in the words themselves. Reverse Amanda's "hideous book" with her previous "horrible novel" and you will see that the line loses punch: "Hideous book" is a stronger pejorative because *hideous* is more specific and extreme and *book* has harsh consonants. This intensification is not accidental. More often, however, the escalating repetitions such as Tom's "I'm going out! . . . Out, out out!" and Amanda's "No, no, no, no, no!" demand a build-up in the actor's delivery. The build-up in these repeated words can be developed in many ways, but they must build. Monotonous delivery of any of these lines would defeat the dramatic impact of the argument and destroy its realism.

Beats, by themselves, do not have structure; they are individual units of each character's part. Tom's beats in the quoted scene might be:

1. "What am I supposed to do?"
2. "You're driving me crazy."
3. "Nothing here is mine."
4. "You are ridiculous."
5. "I pay for the house."
6. "You force me to be a baby."
7. "I'm getting out of here."
8. "Go to hell."

These beats, defined by paraphrases of Tom's thinking (some of which comes out in his lines, some in his actions, some in his laughter and other behavior), are eight separate lines of the attack he pursues with his mother. If the actor can define these lines separately, and recognize their specificity, then Tom's role can be played not as generalized, monolithic rage, but as an

orchestrated build-up of individual grievances coming together
in a dramatic, rather than melodramatic, fury.

Transitions occur quite naturally between subscenes. They do
not necessarily require pauses, or "moments," but pauses are
often effective. In the transition between the first two subscenes,
for example:

AMANDA: . . . you—big—big—IDIOT!

TOM: Look!—I've got *no thing* . . .

Amanda's climax, built by the escalating repetition of *big* and the
all-capitalized and exclamation-pointed *idiot* is a terrifying insult
when delivered from mother to son. It forces Tom to take stock
of just how deeply he has alienated his mother. He might well
take a moment to collect himself, because when he speaks, he
introduces a new argument, one perhaps he has not raised before
but has ruminated about. Clearly, the pause after "Look!" is an
opportunity for Tom to cut back his intensity, to try to speak
calmly instead of shouting. That his mother then accuses him of
shouting becomes all the more revealing, and poignant, and
counter productive, and soon he is back up there, shouting as
before.

There is clearly a moment, and a sudden drop in intensity,
following Laura's desperate cry at the end of the fourth subscene. That she has been drawn into the battle momentarily
stuns both Tom and Amanda, and Amanda is the first to take
advantage of the shock of Laura's cry.

Building to a climax, sharpening transitions, and playing beats
and moments to their fullest potential is the technical side of
good dramatic acting. Technique echoes reality, and it provides
a good shape for dramatic dialog: It brings out the structure of
well-written plays and even gives a sense of structure to poorly
written ones. Finding the structure in a scene is not an easy task,
but the ingredients are known and their outline can be traced.
Being able to define how a scene is put together is a necessary
first step to making the scene *work*; it is necessary, in acting, not
merely to know what a scene is about, or what a character is
about, but how a scene or a character can be made to reveal
what it's about.

EXERCISE 23-1

SCENE STRUCTURE IN ACTION

Learn the *Glass Menagerie* scene with a partner. Follow the breakdown of the scene closely. Subsequently, in class, do the scene *in unison:* all the men playing Tom, all the women playing Amanda. Try to blend in with the majority in terms of rising and falling intensities, the duration of pauses, and the rising/falling inflections. Repeat three times. Then, with a new partner, play the scene "cold."

Did new structural elements assert themselves from the unison experience? Don't try to copy anyone; do try, however, to come to grips with what seem to be universal structural elements in the dialog.

Summary

Scenes are not monolithic; they are structured dramatic material, and defining the structure is part of the actor's task. Scenes can be divided into French scenes, subscenes, beats, and moments, with transitions defining the beginning and end of each. The orchestration of these into a building and climaxing pattern creates dramatic form, builds and sustains audience interest, and delivers an aesthetic "jolt" that is always satisfying and often cathartic. This structure is inherent in a good dramatic text, but much of it is supported by the actor, and much is created by the actor.

Building a Scene

Building and Topping

A scene is built both by the depth of the interplay between actors and by the incorporation of good structural builds in that playing.

The climax of a scene—and the subclimaxes that precede it—are the focal points of the scene. These are the *highs*, in actor parlance, and it is your job to make the most of them.

But structure demands more than climaxes, and a scene that is simply a series of highs becomes a shouting match and little else. In order to have highs you must have lows, and in order to get from lows to highs and back again you must have builds and cutbacks.

Much of the structuring of a scene will come through improvisation and spontaneous rehearsal. But some of it will come through conscious effort. You must be prepared to make that effort.

Build means rising intensity, usually signified by increased volume, increased pitch range (particularly on the high side), and more vigorous physical activity. *Topping* is line-by-line building. A line that tops the previous one is stronger in delivery: usually louder, sharper, angrier (in an argument), and more physical. In a standard build, one line tops another in serial fashion. Actors should feel very comfortable with standard builds, for they are the basic building blocks of most dramatic scenes.

EXERCISE 24–1
STANDARD BUILD I

Play this scene: You are a boxing referee counting out the champion who has just been knocked out by the challenger. Imagine a crowd cheering you on and the challenger dancing excitedly beside you as you count: "One, two, three, four, five, six, seven, eight, nine, ten—and the winner is [use your own name here]!" Make each number more excited than the last.

EXERCISE 24–2
STANDARD BUILD II

Play this scene with your partner. You and a partner are bidding at an auction for something you both dearly want. With each bid, you feel you are getting closer to clinching the sale. Try to top your partner with each bid, and try to win the auction each time.

YOU: Ten dollars.

YOUR PARTNER: Twenty dollars!

YOU: Thirty dollars!

YOUR PARTNER: Forty dollars!

Keep bidding to one hundred dollars, topping each line. Try bidding to two hundred dollars.

EXERCISE 24–3
STANDARD BUILD III

You and a partner exchange the following dialog, topping each other every time.

YOU: Be quiet.

YOUR PARTNER: You be quiet.

YOU: You be quiet.

YOUR PARTNER: You be quiet.

YOU: You be quiet.

YOUR PARTNER: You be quiet!

Try eight exchanges, then ten, then twelve. How far can you go? [But don't destroy your voice!] You can play variations on this build, such as "You will!" "I won't!" or "Yes!" "No!"

In doing those exercises, you quickly see that a straight build cannot go on very long; you quickly reach the top of your vocal range (and in scene acting you would reach the top of an emotional/verbalizing range as well). No further building is possible. There are two techniques to prevent that. The first is to develop more subtle gradations of topping; well-trained actors can "go up the ladder with smaller steps" and can sustain a straight build in finely modulated ways. That ability, of course, requires years of training and experience. The second technique you can put into practice immediately: That is cutting back.

Cutting Back

A cutback is a sudden drop in intensity—at least in expressed intensity—which allows you to start building again. The cutback cannot be arbitrary, however; it must come from some change of approach, and usually from some minor subclimax in the action or argument. The four subscenes of *The Glass Menagerie* studied in Lesson 23 show four builds followed by cutbacks, each build reaching a bit higher than the last. On a larger scale, this is the ordinary pattern of drama.

Each cutback must be tied to some sort of realization, or reconsideration, within the scene itself. In the auction exercise, for example, imagine that after "eighty dollars," you stop bidding, pull out your wallet, check the "secret compartment," and then with a smile whisper "ninety dollars." You have de-escalated the intensity in a classic cutback, from which you and your partner can start the build all over again, climaxing at a final sale of "two hundred dollars" without losing the overall build, or losing your voices.

Getting on Top

Topping the other actor's line—and topping it while leaving both yourself and your partner with somewhere yet to go—is one of the great skills of acting.

Volume and pitch are the first ingredients of getting on top. You can hear that in music, where a composer builds excitement into a score by adding voices, adding instruments, and raising the volume and pitch. Physicalizing is another way: In an American musical, a scene progresses from solo to chorus to solo plus chorus, to "everybody dance" in a classic music theatre build. Listen to some of the great musical builds in music literature: Verdi's "Dies Irae" from the *Requiem* for its rising and apocalyptic exhilaration; Ravel's *Bolero* for its steadily growing sensuality. An actor who could master such builds would be able to achieve near-miracles on stage.

As an actor you can build an argument by becoming more precise, by lengthening the vowels, by getting more reckless, by risking more tactically, by showing more feeling, by loosening your tie, by grabbing a knife, by standing up, by standing on your toes, by stepping forward, by making a noise, by slamming your fist on the table, by "biting" your words, by turning over a piece of furniture, by smashing your glass in the fireplace. Conversely, you can build a seduction scene by getting sultrier and sultrier, by letting your voice grow more and more liquid, your body more senual and evocative, and your actions more and more fetching and charming.

Pacing a Build

Line linkage is crucial in building, since lines that build *must* be springboards for each other. Look at the exchanges between Tom and Amanda in both Lesson 22 and Lesson 23. See how the builds—fairly obvious in each case—evolved from closely linked lines—indeed, from overlapping lines in the second of those scenes. In general, pauses kill builds, and therefore pauses, again in general, should be reserved for transitions and cutbacks.

Accelerating tempos are characteristic of a build; this occasionally means speeding up line delivery, but more often it means speeding up cue pickups. A scene reaching its climax is like an argument reaching its breaking point: Both people are simply *dying* to speak; they can't wait to be *let* into the conversation—they *break in* instead. This accelerated tempo speeds up the blood and induces a recklessness that is also characteristic of the emotional exuberance of climactic confrontations. Think of a bullfight, which reaches its peak of excitement as the bull gets closer and closer to the matador and passes in shorter and shorter (faster and faster) lunges. So does a scene build to its highest level of intensity.

Cutting back the tempo is necessary between subscenes and following climaxes and subclimaxes, but cutting back too quickly and too often is a trap for the beginning actor. Cutting back is unfortunately quite comfortable: It gives you breathing time and thinking time, and as a result young actors often create too many cutbacks. Some beginning actors will cut back on virtually every line. Cutting back often can be justified realistically, of course, but it makes for a poor and uninteresting dramatic structure. You can find reasons to be a bad actor if you look hard enough. If a bull doesn't increase his tempo during a fight, the promoter gets a new bull. If an actor fails the same way in the professional world, the director gets a new actor.

Complex Builds

Straight builds—with escalating volume, rising pitch, and accelerating tempos—cannot be sustained indefinitely, and they cannot simply follow each other like a string of sausages—not even like an ascending string of sausages. In addition to straight builds, the theatre has much more subtle builds that could be called complex.

Complex builds require a change of *tactics* within a build.

EXERCISE 24–4

I DETEST MONDAY

Build the following line: "I detest Monday, Tuesday, Wednesday, Thursday, Friday, Saturday, and Sunday!"

Now build this line: "I adore Monday, Tuesday, Wednesday, Thursday, Friday, Saturday, Sunday."

Notice that building the first line requires a growing sense of displeasure, whereas building the second requires an increased sensitivity and enjoyment. Each line heads toward a different climax or end point. As an actor, you should work to differentiate all seven steps—in both directions—by degree of intensity.

EXERCISE 24–5
I DETEST JANUARY

Substitute months of the year for days of the week, increasing the steps of Exercise 24–4 from seven to twelve.

EXERCISE 24–6
COME HERE

With a partner, build the following exchange:

YOU: Come here.

YOUR PARTNER: No.

YOU: Come here.

YOUR PARTNER: No.

YOU: Come here.

YOUR PARTNER: No.

YOU: Come here.

YOUR PARTNER: No.

You can play the "come here" dialog as a straight build, or you can vary the tactics. In this case, varying the tactics is the best solution if the tactics build. That is, you first invite, then command, then wheedle, then threaten. Or you could invite, wheedle, threaten, and seduce. In either event, the change of tactics permits a varied approach within a straight and continuous build.

Building can also employ a change of rhetoric or tone of voice. A parent arguing with a child will frequently escalate the argument by talking in a louder and lower voice, and by employing the child's full name: "Jonathan Mark Spencer, you come right in here!" Increasing formality, with rising emotional drive, builds a scene. Molière, the French comic dramatist of the seventeenth century (and one of the best dramatic craftsmen of all time) used this device frequently. Look at this straight build of a lovers' quarrel from *The Bourgeois Gentleman* as it shifts from simple banter to the more formal to the overinflated:

BANTER:	Well, then explain.
	No, I've said enough.
	Tell me.
	No, I have nothing to tell.

MORE FORMAL:	Have a heart.
	No.
	I beg you.
	Leave me alone.
	I implore you.
	Go away from me.

OVERINFLATED:	Speak to me!
	Absolutely not!
	Enlighten my suspicions!
	I can't be bothered.
	Ameliorate my anxiety!
	I have no wish to do so.

EXERCISE 24–7
BUILDING MOLIÈRE

Use the speeches from *The Bourgeois Gentleman* to practice building dialog exchanges. Involve your movements and expression, not merely your voice.

Realism

Once again, building is something that happens in life, not just in the theatre. If you are playing for a victory, and you find obstacles in your way, you have to work harder to win what you want. If at first you don't succeed—and you won't, or the play will be over after the first line—then you not only have to try, try again, but you have to try *harder*. Arguments escalate precisely because the other person doesn't agree with you. Seductions intensify because the object of your appeal doesn't immediately run into your arms.

Whatever you strive for in the theatre, you are bound to run into resistance (in dramaturgy it's called conflict); your efforts to overcome the resistance are akin to your efforts to top your partner and thereby build your scenes. Building a scene, then, shows most of all that you *care*. A scene that doesn't build not only seems dramatically flat, it seems to be about someone (you, if you're the culprit) who doesn't care whether he or she wins or loses, who doesn't care about the outcome or winning a victory. The person who cares *will* escalate the arguments and actions, *will* top all objection and counter all resistance, *will* explode right to the climax and catharsis if necessary to get what he or she wants. This intensification is what building requires and what building is; it is not simply a mechanical fact of good dramaturgy, which in this case is only a reflection of deeply felt human interaction.

Summary

Scenes don't just happen—they are built. Building means finding the structure of the scene, and playing the builds up to the subclimaxes and climaxes. Scenes build by increased volume, raised pitch, increased commitment and concern, and accelerated tempos. Experienced actors can make straight builds of infinitely subtle gradations; beginning actors should start the process of learning how to make those small steps toward climactic heights. No builds can be sustained indefinitely, however, so actors must also learn to cut back from time to time, usually between subscenes, after subclimaxes, or both, to give themselves room to build again. Builds can also be varied and complex, building on tactics and tones and rhetorical formulation rather than straight volume, pitch, and intensity. In addition to matching mechanical matters of dramaturgy, building is lifelike. It conveys the impression of characters who care deeply and are committed to victory for their desires.

L'Envoi

L'envoi is a rather quaint literary term for the author's last words —sort of like saying "The ball is now in *your* court." It is also an opportunity for the author to return to the first person, which I now choose to do.

The problems of acting transcend culture, theatrical experience, and educational background; they surface in all actors almost all the time. Good actors lick their problems by training, by craft, by instinct, and by dedication. They put their time where it belongs: in their work. I have never known harder working actors than veteran professionals. The more experienced they are, the more time and effort they put into their acting, and the more serious they are about matters of craft and technique.

The lessons in this book can be covered in a one-year course. Better, they can be explored in some depth in a one-and-a-half or a two-year course, interspersed with scene work. There are some lessons that actors could return to well into their flourishing careers; without question areas touched on here will remain problems for some actors throughout their lives.

To study acting as a humanistic activity, as a means of self-expression and of developing self-confidence, to study the art of theatre as exemplified by the actor and by the acting process: These are laudable goals. To a great extent, they are *my* goals.

To study acting with the idea of making your livelihood as an actor—an artist of the theatre—is an equally laudable goal but an infinitely more difficult one.

My l'envoi is addressed primarily to those actors who want to go on, beyond *Acting One*, to the possibilities of a professional career. This career requires great dedication and sacrifice. The hours are long, the working conditions dreary, the life perplexing, the opportunities few, and the rewards seemingly always around the corner. The pay is bad (when there is pay) and the work is irregular (when there is work). The politics are often pervasive and unfair.

To overcome these conditions you will need a solid acting approach that you can "turn on" in an instant: at an audition, a cold reading, an interview, a rehearsal, or as a hurriedly summoned understudy.

You will need working habits that are concentrated and efficient, and you will need the freedom to employ them twenty-four hours a day—*any* day—when necessary.

You will need an instrument that is the world's best: Lacking that, you need one that is very close to being the world's best. There are only a few hundred career actors, after all; there are hundreds of *thousands* of acting students, community actors, and retired football players and rock stars.

You will need a technique that is fully developed, that goes into operation silently and unconsciously and seems unforced, and that clings to your approach like skin to a snake.

You will need to feel comfortable in periods other than your own, and with styles of speaking, moving, gesturing, and behaving that at first sight seem strange, even ridiculous. You will need to feel comfortable performing in forums quite unlike your acting classroom: in big open amphitheatres, cramped television studios, in-the-round experimental theatres, and in a casting director's office.

You will need to understand different sorts of characters: fat people, thin people, scared people, proud people, rulers, slaves, winners, losers, mutes, mutants. And you will have to learn how much of *you* is in them—and how much of them is in you. And you must learn how to show all this without fear of discovery, but rather with joy in the freedom of your fearlessness.

You will have to know how to manage a career and build an

art at the same time; how to stay fed and intellectually satisfied on a day-to-day and year-to-year basis.

You will need a love for the theatre: for plays as well as playing, for ideas, for words, for deeply drawn characters and feelings, for the rhythm of dialog, for physical expression, for the human body, for poetry, for nuance, for imagery, and for life itself and all that it can teach us.

You will need the most demanding and most exacting standards—for *yourself*—and a willingness to reach for them always.

If you have these things, and also the ineffables of talent and luck, you may have a chance. If you have them in prodigious quantity, you may have a good chance. I certainly wish you well. This book is dedicated to your success.

Index

203